CH00683901

Britain's Railways in Colour

BR Diesels in the 1960s and 1970s

Haynes Publishing

Britain's Railways in Colour

BR Diesels in the 1960s and 1970s

Colin G. Maggs MBE

© Colin G. Maggs, 2010

All rights reserved. No part of this publication may be reproduced,
stored in a retrieval system or transmitted, in any form or by
any means, electronic, mechanical, photocopying, recording or
otherwise, without prior permission in writing from the publisher.

First published in August 2010
Reprinted January 2011

A catalogue record for this book is available
from the British Library

ISBN 978 1 84425 651 8

Library of Congress catalog card no. 2010924920

Design and layout by Dominic Stickland

Haynes North America Inc., 861 Lawrence Drive,
Newbury Park, California 91320, USA

Published by Haynes Publishing,
Sparkford, Yeovil, Somerset BA22 7JJ, UK.
Tel: 01963 442030 Fax: 01963 440001
Int. tel: +44 1963 442030
Int. fax: +44 1963 440001
E-mail: sales@haynes.co.uk
Website: www.haynes.co.uk

Printed and bound in the USA by Odcombe Press LP,
1299 Bridgestone Parkway, La Vergne, TN 37086

ACKNOWLEDGEMENTS

Special thanks are due to Colin Roberts for checking the text and
amplifying the captions.

Colin G. Maggs MBE, 2010

Contents

Introduction

The photographs in this book were taken either by myself, or by my friends, including the Reverend Alan Newman, whose transparencies are now in my care. We all lived in or near Bath, so the area covered by the pictures is therefore weighted towards the southern half of England, although we made some occasional forays into the splendid northern climes. Unfortunately Classes 20 and 40 escaped our attention.

In the 1960s and '70s, the attitude of railway photographers towards colour was totally different from today. Now, a cameraman taking a colour picture will know that if it is reproduced in a book, journal or newspaper, it will appear in colour. Not so in those days when colour printing was much more expensive than black and white (monochrome), which meant most reproductions were in b&w. Monochrome film was cheaper and had the additional advantage of being 'faster', whereas colour film in those days was very 'slow' and therefore not so good for capturing trains at speed.

These facts meant that black and white was the principal format, but some enthusiasts used a second camera loaded with colour film, just for their own private, or railway society viewing in mind, rather than for publication.

Also at that time, some very narrow-minded photographers considered diesel locomotives to be the 'murderers of steam locomotives' and refused to take images of them! Others believed that they were not so photogenic as steam engines and so pictures of them were not worth taking.

During the decade of change from steam to diesel and electric traction, the railways saw a multitude of other changes, so it was the whole railway scene which became different, not just the motive power. These included the following features:

- the closure of less-busy stations and branch lines;
- the singling of some lesser-used main lines;
- the almost complete abolition of mechanical signalling and its replacement by centrally controlled colour lights;
- modern gravity shunting yards were made redundant as trains became mostly of fixed formation;
- shunting anywhere became almost a thing of the past as a train carried one type of load rather than mixed freight (the development of the motorway network about this time had enabled small loads to be transported quickly by road);
- the closure of many engine sheds (which had the drawback that in the event of an engine failure, a replacement often had to be sent for from a considerable distance);
- lineside telephone wires and poles were removed;
- a livery different from steam days was adopted in order to promote a new image;
- a passenger train consisted of a fixed set of vehicles – although this gave a better use of coaches, it offered no flexibility when there was a surge of passengers;
- a decrease was experienced in the number of summer Saturday trains;
- the diesel multiple unit (dmu) was introduced which proved very useful at intermediate stations where reversal was required, eg on the Cardiff to Portsmouth service there was now no need to run an engine round at Bristol Temple Meads, the driver simply walking from one end of the train to the other;
- coaches were now heated by electricity rather than steam and became air-braked, rather than by vacuum;
- wagons were braked from the locomotive, so brake vans and a guard at the rear of a train were no longer necessary;
- luggage handling at stations became mainly self-service rather than using a porter;
- gas and oil lighting disappeared from stations;
- railway collection and delivery of parcels was abolished;
- livestock was no longer carried by rail, resulting in closure of associated infrastructure such as cattle docks;
- some stations, formerly manned, became unstaffed when pay-trains were introduced – harking back to the days of the rail motor and the auto train;
- a startling contrast could be seen between the appearance of steam and diesel locomotive sheds: the former were dark and dirty, but the latter so clean you could almost eat off the floor and they were brightly lit;
- the abolition of the steam locomotive rendered water columns, tanks, water troughs and turntables obsolete.

BR classified its diesel locomotives by horsepower, from 1956 giving each class a Type No.

Type	Engine horsepower
1	800–1,000
2	1,001–1,499
3	1,500–1,999
4	2,000–2,999
5	3,000+

TOPS

BR introduced a computer system in 1973–75 for recording all locomotives and rolling stock, and their movements, the Total Operations Processing System, known as TOPS. This resulted in the reclassification and renumbering of locomotives and multiple units, ranging from the smallest shunters, Classes 01 and 02, to the most powerful diesel locomotives of the time, the Class 55 'Deltics'. Not all classes survived long enough to receive their TOPS numbers, which are prefixed with the class number. Based on an American system it was introduced in Britain an area at a time and is still in use today.

I have interpreted the title liberally and a few pictures date from the 1950s, and to set diesel locomotives in context, I have included a few views depicting electric traction and one gas turbine locomotive. This book is arranged generally, with the most powerful locomotives first, followed by multiple units. Illustrations are in locomotive or multiple unit numerical order within a class and have been selected to show a variety of liveries, duties and locations.

This collection is intended to be savoured again and again, and just as with a painting, you are invited to come back and see fresh things and are not expected to take it all in at one quick glance.

A brief summary of BR diesel developments in the 1960s and '70s

Arguably, the most innovative post-war traction development up to 1960 was the 90mph 'Blue Pullman' dmus. A power car at each end allowed a rapid turn-round at termini – no shunting was required to and from carriage sidings. The five sets built by Metropolitan-Cammell were luxurious, with armchair seats and full air-conditioning, but unfortunately, poor bogie design gave a rough ride at times. The 'Blue Pullmans' were withdrawn in 1973 after a relatively short life, with none of the 36 vehicles surviving, but the basic principle was excellent and the High Speed Train (HST), the 'InterCity125', entered service in 1975, which was clearly a development of this concept.

The 22 production 'Deltics' were another great innovation. Capable of 100mph they reduced the London to Edinburgh time from seven to six hours and Leeds to three – the same as in pre-Second World War days, but with ordinary passenger trains, not just a prestige service.

The familiar BR twin-track/double arrow logo was introduced in 1964 and passenger stock started to appear in a livery of blue and light grey. The West Coast electrification was introduced in April 1966, using a 'clockface' (regular interval) timetable and many trains averaged 80mph. The number of passengers increased due to what is referred to as the 'sparks effect' phenomenon of electrification.

The railway underwent many changes in the 1960s, the most notable of which was of course the abolition of steam traction in August 1968 but also signalling was centralised in many areas; hundreds of goods yards closed; long lengths of flat-bottomed rail led to less maintenance and obviated the need for local permanent way gangs.

Probably the finest achievement of the 1970s, however, was the HST as mentioned above. It offered a stable and almost uncannily silent ride at 125mph and was fitted with disc brakes which had the economic advantage that the existing signalling system could be retained: had the brakes not been so efficient, at high speeds the distance between signals would have needed to have been increased to allow sufficient distance to bring a train to a standstill. Production HSTs were introduced on the Western Region in October 1976 and on the East Coast Main Line two years later, resulting in the cascading and withdrawal of many diesel locomotives. Track improvements were made to allow HSTs to run at high speeds – such as the 118½ miles from Bristol Temple Meads to Paddington, in 1½ hours. Travelling by HST, unlike the 'Blue Pullman', carried no supplement and competed favourably in journey time with a car travelling on a motorway.

Colin G. Maggs MBE
August 2010

Main line diesel locomotives

Class 55 'Deltic'
English Electric Type 5 Co-Co diesel-electric

22 built, introduced 1961–2 Nos D9000–D9021
(TOPS Nos 55001–55022)

The *Deltic* prototype, now to be seen in Locomotion, the National Railway Museum at Shildon, was built by English Electric at its Dick Kerr Works, Preston, to use a development of the Napier opposed-piston two-stroke engine as supplied to the Admiralty for use in fast, small craft such as motor torpedo boats. The locomotive weighed only 106 tons, yet produced 3,300hp compared with the two LMS 127½-ton locomotives, Nos 10000 and 10001, each providing only 1,600hp, or the Southern Region 135-ton Nos 102010–10203, also producing 1,600hp. *Deltic*, also known as DP1 (diesel prototype No. 1) had a maximum speed of 100mph, but it was only the Eastern Region which saw the value of this twin-engine design. Objections were that it was more expensive to buy than other diesel-electric locomotives, and was a more complex machine. The cost was £150,000 each, rather than about £125,000 for a Brush Type 4.

The 22 production locomotives weighed only 99 tons each, and after running-in, entered service with the introduction of the June 1962 timetable. In the interest of economy, its bogies were the same design as those of the English Electric Type 3, later Class 37.

Although from 1978, trains on the East Coast Main Line, formerly hauled by 'Deltics', were replaced by HSTs, in the 1979 timetable a 'Deltic' had the honour of working BR's fastest ever locomotive-hauled train, the 17.05 'Hull Executive' from King's Cross, when the 138½ miles to Retford were booked at an average speed of 91.32mph.

A unique and highly detailed contract was put in place on 28 March 1958 between BR and the manufacturer for five years from delivery of the first locomotive. Maintenance would be carried out by BR under the supervision of English Electric, but EE would overhaul major components at its expense, as detailed in appendices of the contract. EE was contracted to ensure the 22 locomotives would be available to run 4½ million miles per year, but no individual locomotive was to run more than 220,000 per annum. In operation, the Class 55s proved very reliable. They were withdrawn at the beginning of 1982, of which six, plus the prototype, survive.

⬆ No. 9003 *Meld* at King's Cross on 28 May 1968. The BR double-arrow logo and the shortening of British Railways to British Rail was introduced in the summer of 1964. This locomotive has had the 'D' prefix removed from its number as unnecessary since there was no likelihood of it being confused with remaining steam engines. The signalbox looms large in the background. (It is believed that the '15B' sign either refers to a speed restriction of 15mph over route B, or is applicable to dmus which were Class B passenger trains.) *(Rev. Alan Newman)*

⬆ No. D9007 *Pinza* at Clarence Yard, the King's Cross stabling point, on 1 June 1967. It is in the original two-tone green livery but with yellow ends. Sheltering behind it, left, is the similar-looking No. DP2, which was the forerunner of the EE Class 50s. It had an English Electric 2,700hp engine giving a maximum tractive effort of 50,000lb and was clothed in a 'Deltic' bodyshell. No. DP2 was destroyed in a serious accident at Thirsk a couple of months after this picture was taken. In the background, right, is the entrance to Gasworks Tunnel. *(Rev. Alan Newman)*

⬇ No. D9008 *The Green Howards* (left) and No. DP2 at King's Cross on 1 June 1967 with a Brush Type 4 on the far right. A rake of diesel fuel tank wagons is behind No. DP2. In the centre of the picture, between the tracks, is a lightweight permanent way trolley designed so that it can be easily put on or taken off the rails. *(Rev. Alan Newman)*

⬆ No. D9014 *The Duke of Wellington's Regiment* heads an up express at Hadley Wood on 14 October 1968, passing a three-car dmu to its left. *(Rev. Alan Newman)*

⬇ No. 9015 *Tulyar* is also seen at Hadley Wood, with an up express on 13 October 1969. The retaining wall on the right kept back the soil when widening altered the slope of the cutting. *Tulyar* has been preserved by the Deltic Preservation Society at Barrow Hill. *(Rev. Alan Newman)*

⬆ No. 50024 is seen west of Bradford-on-Avon with the 09.45 Paddington to Bristol Temple Meads on a Sunday diversion, 18 August 1974. It has full-front warning panel and window frames in yellow. It was later named *Vanguard*. *(Rev. Alan Newman)*

Class 50
English Electric Type 4 Co-Co diesel-electric

50 built, introduced 1967–8, Nos D400–D449
(TOPS Nos 50001–50050)

The Class 50 was the production version of the 'DP2' prototype described earlier. It had a 2,700hp EE engine and weighed 117 tons and had a maximum speed of 100mph. Two new features were rheostatic braking and electronic control of the tractive effort to correct any wheelslip. Up to and including this class, all BR diesel-electric locomotives had been equipped with direct current generators. From the outset, they were fitted with electric train heating equipment.

They were used initially for express working between Euston and Glasgow, until the overhead wires reached Glasgow in 1974, when the entire class was transferred to the Western Region. The latter experienced difficulties with the traction motors as the engines were not happy running fast without a break, for on the West Coast Main Line speed restrictions for subsidence etc. had allowed them a 'breather'.

When they arrived on the WR the Class 50s were in a poor state mechanically and were unreliable. Between 1979 and 1983 they were modified: the rheostatic braking was removed and the inertia filters substituted with banks of filters similar to those used in Class 56 locomotives and HST power cars. The slow-speed control required for merry-go-round working was removed, as was the facility for selecting a tractive effort during acceleration. When working on the WR they were not repaired at Swindon, but went to various places such as Longsight for major attention. They were all given names from famous warships during 1978.

HSTs soon ousted the Class 50 from former GWR lines and from 12 May 1980 some worked between Waterloo and Exeter, chopping 12 minutes off the Salisbury to Exeter run. Others were utilised on the North East–South West route via Birmingham until they were again ousted by HSTs. All were withdrawn by mid-1992 and 18 of the 50 locomotives survive today in preservation.

⬆ No. 50028 pauses at Bath Spa heading the 14.45 Paddington to Weston-super-Mare on 22 June 1974. The steep hill in the background is Beechen Cliff which the author climbed twice daily to reach his grammar school. The church above No. 50028 is St Mark's where the author had the dubious honour of playing the organ for the very last Evensong before it was closed for religious services. The locomotive was later named *Tiger*. *(Rev. Alan Newman)*

↗ No. 50030 passes the site of Hampton Row Halt, east of Bath, heading a Paddington to Bristol Temple Meads express on 13 June 1974. The halt was closed on 25 April 1917 as a wartime economy measure and never reopened. Later named *Repulse*, this Class 50 has been preserved at Peak Rail, Derbyshire. *(Rev. Alan Newman)*

➡ No. 50038 approaches Bath Spa with the 14.15 Paddington to Bristol Temple Meads on 22 June 1974. The red and white checkerboard on the left warns of limited lineside clearance. The bridge parapet to the right is unfortunately at platform height and during the blackout in the Second World War, a sailor on a train too long for the platform, stepped on to this parapet and fell into the river. Fortunately, he lived to tell the tale. To the right of the engine was a small turntable serving very short sidings into which wagons were drawn by a shunting horse. No. 50038 became *Formidable* in May 1978. *(Rev. Alan Newman)*

Classes 45 and 46 'Peak'
BR Sulzer Type 4 1Co-Co1 diesel-electric

183 built, introduced 1960–1, Nos D11–D193
(TOPS Nos 45001–45077; 45101–45150 and 46001–46056)

The initial batch of ten locomotives of this BR design, Nos D1–D10 (later TOPS Class 44 Nos 44001–44010), were equipped with a 2,300hp 12-cylinder Sulzer engine with two banks of six vertical cylinders, each with a separate crankshaft, but coupled to a common output shaft. These were followed by No. D11 onwards (later becoming Classes 45 and 46), which were fitted with a similar engine, but inter-cooled and uprated to 2,500hp. Those from No. D138 were equipped with Brush electrical equipment in place of Crompton Parkinson, and became Class 46. Both the latter classes had a maximum speed of 90mph but weighed a massive 135 tons. Originally all were fitted with a boiler for train steam heating, but a batch was converted with electric train supply (ETS) and classified 45/1 (Nos 45101–45150).

The nose at each end served two purposes: it housed a traction motor for the adjacent bogie and also avoided the driver suffering from 'sleeper flicker' as it prevented him from seeing nearby sleepers passing under the locomotive. The bogies had plate frames like the first SR diesels. Initially, the 'Peaks' were mainly seen on the London Midland Region, all three similar classes taking this name from the first ten Class 44s which were named after English and Welsh mountains.

⬆ No. D12 (later No. 45011) is seen at Ais Gill with an express heading from Glasgow towards Leeds and St Pancras on 12 June 1967. Later TOPS Class 45, it is in green livery with a small yellow warning panel and still has connecting end doors with old-type headcode boxes. The bridge wall behind the signal, left, has been whitened to assist sighting. There is a mixture of rolling stock liveries. *(Rev. Alan Newman)*

⬉ No. D15 (later No. 45018) ticks over at Bath Green Park depot on 18 March 1966. It has drawn out BR Standard Class 5 4-6-0 No. 73001 for scrap, on its way to Messrs Cashmore, Newport; its motion has not been dismantled for towing. The shunter and loco crew discuss the move. No. 73001 had been withdrawn on 31 December 1965 and then reinstated on 1 January 1966 before final withdrawal from service on 8 January 1966. The Somerset & Dorset line closed on 7 March 1966 and from that date the Mangotsfield to Bath line became a long siding, remaining open for coal traffic until Bath gas works closed in 1971. The gas lamps, left, have been raised to offer better lighting and a loading gauge can be seen in the distance. *(Rev. Alan Newman)*

⬅ No. D24 (later No. 45027) basks in the sun at Bristol Temple Meads on 30 April 1966. It has blanked-off nose-end connecting doors, split headcode boxes, and displays a small yellow warning panel. On the right is Brush Type 4 No. D1825 and 'Hymek' No. D7004. *(Rev. Alan Newman)*

⬆ No. D29 (later No. 45002) near Bradford Junctions on 13 September 1971 heading the 10.25 Manchester to Penzance diverted from its usual path due to a derailment at Flax Bourton. It is about to pass under Ladydown Aqueduct which carries the Kennet & Avon Canal over the railway. The Class 45 has a full yellow end for greater visibility as opposed to the small panel of earlier years. *(Rev. Alan Newman)*

⬆ No. 31 (later No. 45030) at Bristol Temple Meads in its new blue livery and without the 'D' prefix, as by this date, 1 September 1969, all BR steam locomotives had been withdrawn for over a year. It heads the 10.35 to Newcastle, and to the left is the 'Bristol Pullman'. *(Rev. Alan Newman)*

↗ No. D52 (later No. 45123) *The Lancashire Fusilier*, complete with regimental badge, while beyond is Brush Type 4 No. D1966, this number being apt for the year of the photograph, which was taken at Bristol Bath Road Depot on 30 April. *(Rev. Alan Newman)*

➡ No. D65 (later No. 45111) *Grenadier Guardsman*, also with a regimental badge, stands with 'Hymek' No. D7022 at Bristol Bath Road depot on 1 June 1966. The water tank is for replenishing diesel locomotive steam heating boilers. *(Rev. Alan Newman)*

← No. 68 (later No. 45046) heads the 07.35 Sheffield to the West of England express on 20 April 1970, viewed from Puxton Crossing signalbox, with a wicket gate to the right of the main level crossing gate. This allowed foot passengers to cross the line after the main gates had been closed, and when a train approached, the signalman pulled a lever to lock the pedestrian gate. Lighting is still by gas. *(Rev. Alan Newman)*

↑ No. 75 (later No. 45052) in blue livery and Brush No. 1599 in two-tone green, rest at Bristol Bath Road shed on 23 April 1969. *(Rev. Alan Newman)*

↓ No. D83 (later No. 45142) approaches Bradford-on-Avon with the up afternoon parcels train on 10 July 1967. *(Rev. Alan Newman)*

No. 110 (later No. 45065) heads an up van train at Salisbury on 15 May 1973. To the right is the brick building formerly the GWR passenger train shed. It was near this spot where an up boat train from Plymouth derailed on the sharp curve on 1 July 1906 with considerable loss of life. The 'banner' type of signal is supported on a length of recycled rail. *(Rev. Alan Newman)*

No. D115 (later No. 45067) crosses the river west of Bradford-on-Avon on 16 May 1966. There is a 40mph speed restriction sign and the two rusty inner rails are to prevent a derailed vehicle from plunging into the water. *(Rev. Alan Newman)*

No. D122 (later No. 45070) in green livery with small yellow warning panel, leaves Bristol Temple Meads with the 10.40 to Newcastle on 2 September 1968. It is using one of the platforms added in 1935 when the train shed, right, proved to offer inadequate accommodation. Adjacent to the engine, right, are Royal Mail carts. *(Rev. Alan Newman)*

⬆ No. D161 (later No. 46024) with the Saturdays-only 15.48 Bristol Temple Meads to Weymouth, approaching Freshford on 29 August 1970. Four coaches are in blue and grey livery, but that nearest the engine is in the older maroon style. Locomotives from No. D138 onwards were fitted with Brush traction motors instead of the Crompton Parkinson type and under the TOPS system became Class 46. Freshford is one of the few village stations still open in 2010. *(Rev. Alan Newman)*

↗ No. D165 (later No. 46028) emits a cloud of exhaust by Bristol Temple Meads Loco Yard signalbox on 23 April 1969. This box opened on 10 December 1934 and was closed on 17 March 1970. *(Rev. Alan Newman)*

➡ No. D187 (later No. 46050) works an up mixed freight east of Bath on 10 June 1968. In the first part of the consist are five 21-ton hopper wagons branded 'House Coal Concentration'. Collieries did not always keep records up to date and sometimes despatched coal to stations still open for goods traffic but closed for coal as it had been concentrated at one central depot. *(Rev. Alan Newman)*

◥ No. 45047 (originally No. D69) draws out of Totnes on 28 August 1975 throwing up an exhaust plume. The signal posts carry diamonds indicating the track is circuited and that the signalman will be aware of the train's presence. No. 45047 is about to tackle Rattery Incline with gradients as steep as 1 in 46. Four milk tank wagons are for use by the nearby creamery, which closed in 2008, but by then had not been rail-connected for some years. *(Rev. Alan Newman)*

◅ No. 45058 (originally No. D97) climbs the 1 in 146 from Yate South Junction to join the South Wales main line, with a North to West of England train on 30 May 1977. Note the post indicating 120½ miles from Derby. *(Rev. Alan Newman)*

◩ No. 46004 (originally No. D141) emerges from the goods loop at Bathampton with an up freight on 10 May 1978. The centre part of the train appears to consist of engineer's department wagons. *(Rev. Alan Newman)*

Classes 42 and 43 'Warship'
BR and North British Type 4 B-B diesel-hydraulic

71 built, introduced 1958–62, Nos D800–D832 and D866–D870
(BR Class 42) and Nos D833–D865 (North British Class 43)

BR Western Region engineers saw Germany using hydraulic rather than electric transmission and were impressed by the fact that it was lighter and thus gave an excellent power/weight ratio. The North British company built five A1A-A1A 'Warships' in 1958 (Class 41 Nos D600–D604), the later BR and North British-built design being B-B. Two engines were fitted to each locomotive producing a total horsepower of 2,000, 2,200, or 2,400, depending on their rating. Their maximum speed was 90mph and they were fitted for steam heating. Diesel-hydraulic locomotives cost less than a diesel-electric of the same power, and because of the lighter weight, had a haulage capacity of two coaches more per train than a 'Peak'.

For the first three years of their lives, the diesel-hydraulics performed well, but then the hydraulic transmission started giving trouble. A single hydraulic transmission unit was unable to handle more than about 2,000hp, so each locomotive had two sets of transmissions.

The Maybach engines (BR-built locomotives) and MAN engines (North British-built), were of complex design, making overhaul and repair expensive. Furthermore, a diesel-hydraulic locomotive requires about three times the capital value in spares than a comparable diesel-electric. Another drawback was that when the locomotives were first ordered, it was the policy to fit all freight wagons with continuous brakes, but this order was rescinded for a while when it was found to be too costly. This meant that the relatively light 'Warships' lacked sufficient braking power on their eight wheels to control an unbraked train. Meanwhile, electrical engineers had produced lighter traction motors and generators, thus taking away the advantage of a diesel-hydraulic's lighter weight.

As the mileage of a 'Warship' increased its riding qualities decreased and by early 1960 they were restricted to a maximum of 80mph. The Class 42s also worked the Waterloo–Exeter expresses latterly, but the swansong of the 'Warships' was the acceleration of the Paddington to Plymouth service in the summer 1968 timetable. Four pairs of Maybach-engined locomotives worked extra fast trains in pairs. Shortage of spares caused problems and by the beginning of 1971 the practice of them working the 'Cornish Riviera Express' in pairs was abandoned. The final 'Warships' were withdrawn in late 1972, with just two Class 42s being preserved.

↑ No. D804 *Avenger* is seen at Westbury on 20 May 1966. The semaphore signalling here was to last another 18 years. *(Rev. Alan Newman)*

↖ No. D807 *Caradoc* heads an up mixed freight at Bradford-on-Avon on 3 November 1966. *(Rev. Alan Newman)*

← No. D810 *Cockade* waits at Westbury with an up train on 16 September 1966. The signals are worthy of a second glance. *(Rev. Alan Newman)*

↑ Another view of No. D810 *Cockade* as it passes through Salisbury with a down working on 20 May 1966 while 350hp shunter No. D3013 stands on the left. *(Rev. Alan Newman)*

↑ Nos 815 *Druid* and 867 *Zenith* are seen dumped at Marsh Junction, Bristol, on 29 October 1971. *(Rev. Alan Newman)*

↗ No. D823 *Hermes* in maroon livery leaves Salisbury with a train to Waterloo on 20 May 1966. *(Rev. Alan Newman)*

→ Nos D826 *Jupiter* and D868 *Zephyr* pull out from Westbury with the 14.30 Plymouth to Paddington service on 3 June 1968. They are in their final livery colour of BR blue, following their original Brunswick green and later maroon. The line on the left curves round to Trowbridge. *(Rev. Alan Newman)*

↑ Nos D827 *Kelly* and D869 *Zest* wait by Westbury North signalbox while double-heading the 14.30 Plymouth to Paddington on 26 July 1968. No. D869 is in the earlier maroon livery while No. D827 has been repainted in BR corporate blue with double-arrow symbols on the cab sides, beneath the numbers. In the station, a Class 33 heads a train of hopper wagons. *(Rev. Alan Newman)*

↗ No. 827 *Kelly* again, terminates at Westbury with the 09.50 from Weymouth on 29 November 1971. It now carries a single arrow emblem on its bodyside. *(Rev. Alan Newman)*

→ No. D831 *Monarch* leaves Avonmouth with a freight on 8 February 1967. When two arrow emblems were used, the numbers were usually repositioned to the ends of the bodysides as seen here. *(Rev. Alan Newman)*

38 BR Diesels in the 1960s and 1970s

← Nos D831 *Monarch* and D808 *Centaur* at Westbury double-head the 14.30 Plymouth to Paddington on 30 July 1968. They show the difference in number positions, even when carrying double-arrows symbols on the cabsides, being either on the bodyside or cabsides. The second locomotive has a full-front yellow end including window frames, while the first displays a small yellow warning panel. The lines on the right once served an iron foundry. *(Rev. Alan Newman)*

↑ No. D831 *Monarch* again, as it passes Westmoreland Road Yard, Bath, with a down freight on 13 February 1968. Two brake vans can be seen towards the centre of the train. Although the yard closed to goods in May 1967, it remained open for full-load traffic until 31 December 1980. One siding was taken over for the local authority's refuse terminal, the first train to Calvert, Buckinghamshire, leaving there on 18 November 1985. *(Rev. Alan Newman)*

⬆ Maroon-liveried No. D834 *Pathfinder* heads a freight consisting of vans and 16-ton mineral wagons west of Bradford-on-Avon on 21 September 1966. This was one of the North British-built 'Warships' (later Class 43), which were fitted with two NBL/MAN diesel engines instead of a pair of Bristol Siddeley-Maybach units as fitted to the BR-built 'Warships' (Class 42). The North British locomotives were 1½ tons heavier. *(Rev. Alan Newman)*

↗ North British-built No. D839 *Relentless* is seen in maroon livery at Bristol Bath Road depot on 23 April 1969. A Brush Class 47 is to the left and a 'Western' stands just outside the shed, right. *(Rev. Alan Newman)*

➡ No. D847 *Strongbow* passes Avoncliff Halt with a train of Portishead to Radstock coal empties on 5 November 1970. On 15 August 1966, the 2½ miles between Radstock and Mells Road were closed, Radstock coal being sent out via Bristol. In June 1968, it was decided to reopen this section and close the 14 miles from Radstock to Bristol. This meant that the rail distance from Radstock to Bristol was then 30 miles. The final coal train left Radstock on 16 November 1973, but the track was not lifted as it served a wagon works at Radstock until the late 1980s. Stone trains continue to run on the section from the main line connection at Frome to Hapsford Junction east of Mells Road, and on to Whatley Quarry. *(Rev. Alan Newman)*

← No. D865 *Zealous*, the last of the North British-built 'Warships', catches the afternoon sun at Bradford-on-Avon while heading a down freight on 15 November 1967.
(Rev. Alan Newman)

↑ No. D869 *Zest*, built by BR at Swindon Works in 1961, powers the 16.45 Bristol Temple Meads to Westbury through Trowbridge on 10 July 1971. None of the 'Warships' survived in traffic to receive their TOPS numbers in the 42xxx or 43xxx series.
(Rev. Alan Newman)

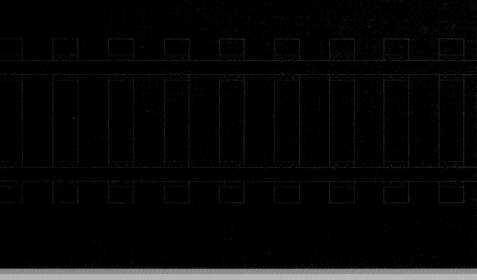

Class 52 'Western' BR Type 4 C-C diesel-hydraulic

74 built, introduced 1961–3, Nos D1000–D1073

The 'Western' class with two Maybach MD655 1,350hp engines were the most powerful and perhaps the most successful BR diesel-hydraulic design, displacing the 'Warships' on most top express duties. In 1961, one Crewe-built 'Western' locomotive cost £135,000, but the price of its diesel-electric equivalent, a Brush Type 4 (now Class 47), also built at Crewe, was approximately £125,000 and the Brush tared at only 6 tons more.

Diesel locomotives were less visible and audible than steam, as well as often travelling faster, so vivid yellow warning panels were added, and clashing with the green livery, disfigured a locomotive's face. The first of the class, No. D1000, was outshopped in what was described as desert sand livery in the hope that it would prove more conspicuous, while No. D1001 was turned out in maroon. Nos D1003 and D1004 were green, but from then on, Swindon-built examples came out in maroon and those from Crewe in green. Finally, maroon was applied to match the passenger rolling stock until BR blue was adopted universally in the mid-1960s.

As the 'Western' bogie was of similar design to that of a 'Warship', riding problems were experienced and 'Westerns' were eventually limited to a maximum of 80mph. They replaced the GWR 'King' class 4-6-0s on the express services and although expected to be ousted in 1975, the slow delivery of HSTs resulted in the last five 'Westerns' not being withdrawn until February 1977. Seven have survived into preservation.

⬆ No. D1007 *Western Talisman* passes Westmoreland Yard, Bath, on
7 February 1969 with the 11.15 Bristol Temple Meads to Paddington.
(Rev. Alan Newman)

No. D1010 *Western Campaigner* hauls LMS 4-6-2 No. 6229 *Duchess of Hamilton* from Minehead to Swindon on 17 March 1975, it having been extricated from static display at Butlin's holiday camp. Later restored for use on the main line, No. 6229 has now been returned to its original streamlined condition for static display at the National Railway Museum, York. No. D1010 has also survived into preservation and, coincidentally, is now based on the Minehead branch, which is operated as the West Somerset Railway. *(Rev. Alan Newman)*

No. D1020 *Western Hero* emerges from Twerton Tunnel on 16 June 1964 with the down 'Bristol Pullman'. The 'Blue Pullman' was undergoing servicing and so was replaced by locomotive-hauled stock on this occasion. *(Author)*

No. D1028 *Western Hussar* waits at Bath Green Park station with the 12.25 to Bristol Temple Meads on 23 October 1965. The locomotive's paintwork is not in the best condition. The former Midland Railway Green Park station closed on 7 March 1966 along with the Somerset & Dorset line to Bournemouth, but the train shed has been preserved and can be enjoyed today. *(Author)*

48 BR Diesels in the 1960s and 1970s

No. D1037 *Western Empress* rests at Midland Bridge Road goods depot, Bath, on 12 December 1968 near the site of the former Somerset & Dorset engine shed, having worked a coal train to Bath gas works. *(Rev. Alan Newman)*

No. D1040 *Western Queen* passes Hawkeridge Junction, Westbury, with coal empties to Radstock on 17 February 1969. The line on the right avoids Westbury station. *(Rev. Alan Newman)*

No. D1040 *Western Queen* again, in maroon livery, heads westwards through Bradford-on-Avon with a coal train from Radstock to Portishead on 5 March 1969. *(Rev. Alan Newman)*

⬆ Another view of No. D1040 *Western Queen*, this time at Bathampton as it draws coal empties from Portishead to Radstock, on 7 March 1969. *(Rev. Alan Newman)*

↗ No. D1044 *Western Duchess* heads out of Westbury with the 08.30 Paignton to Paddington on 5 April 1969, passing the junction of the line to Trowbridge. *(Rev. Alan Newman)*

➡ No. D1045 *Western Viscount* approaches Avondale Road Bridge, Bath, with the midday freight from Bath on 28 May 1969. The empty coal wagons have come from Bath gas works. Beyond the rear of the train was the erstwhile Weston station. The rails of the down road had recently been lifted. *(Rev. Alan Newman)*

⬅ No. D1048 *Western Lady* runs alongside the sea wall near Dawlish Warren with a down express on 21 August 1975. This locomotive has been preserved at the Midland Railway, Butterley. *(Rev. Alan Newman)*

⬆ Blue-liveried No. D1047 *Western Lord* passes Clink Road Junction, Frome, on 25 September 1970 with down stone empties bound for Foster Yeoman's Merehead Quarry. The train is completely vacuum fitted because there is no brake van at the rear, although one can be seen towards the middle of the consist. The hopper wagons are of varying capacities.
(Rev. Alan Newman)

↑ No. D1050 *Western Ruler* in blue livery, enters Westbury with the 09.30 Paddington to Paignton on 5 April 1969. Destination panels hang on the coach sides, this feature having a very short life. *(Rev. Alan Newman)*

↓ Two months later, and No. D1050 *Western Ruler* heads the 11.15 Bristol Temple Meads to Paddington at Broughton Gifford having been diverted via Bradford Junctions on 8 June 1969. This line was singled from 26 February 1967. *(Rev. Alan Newman)*

↗ No. D1051 *Western Ambassador* is seen at Bristol Bath Road depot, 23 April 1969. To the right is an ENPARTS van – the code name for 'engine parts'. The 'Westerns', Class 52 under TOPS, retained their cast number plates until the end, not being renumbered in the 52xxx series, although some had the 'D' chiselled off when the prefix was abolished. *(Rev. Alan Newman)*

↘ No. D1052 *Western Viceroy*, looking a little travel-weary, is seen at Clink Road Junction, Frome, with the 09.30 Paddington to Paignton on 25 September 1970. The red line along the top of the first coach denotes that it contains a buffet; a yellow line indicated first-class accommodation. *(Rev. Alan Newman)*

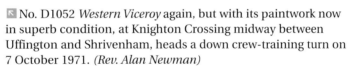

No. D1052 *Western Viceroy* again, but with its paintwork now in superb condition, at Knighton Crossing midway between Uffington and Shrivenham, heads a down crew-training turn on 7 October 1971. *(Rev. Alan Newman)*

No. D1058 *Western Nobleman* passes Fairwood Junction signalbox with the 09.30 Paddington to Paignton on 17 February 1969. The Westbury avoiding line is on the right. *(Rev. Alan Newman)*

No. D1058 *Western Nobleman*, this time on the single-line section between Staverton and Bradford Junctions, in charge of the Royal Train on 9 August 1973. *(Rev. Alan Newman)*

⬉ No. D1067 *Western Druid* passes Bradford Junctions with an Etruria to St Blazey china clay empties working on 22 March 1970. *(Rev. Alan Newman)*

⬅ No. D1072 *Western Glory* is captured near Badminton with a Paddington to South Wales express on 10 April 1976. *(Rev. Alan Newman)*

⬆ No. D1060 *Western Dominion* passes Bathampton signalbox with the 08.45 Paddington to Bristol Temple Meads on 17 April 1969. The line on the right curves sharply to Westbury. The signalbox opened on 21 September 1956 to replace one on the opposite side of the line. Midway along the front of the box is a square plate showing its identification as a two-letter code. With the introduction of MAS signalling it closed on 17 August 1970. The junction signals are particularly interesting: the post is low so that its sighting is not blocked by a bridge, and because of limited space, the arms are on central pivots. *(Rev. Alan Newman)*

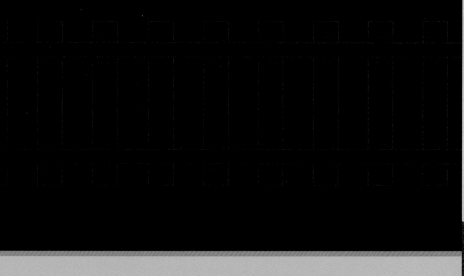

Class 47 BR/Brush Type 4 Co-Co diesel-electric

512 built, introduced 1962–7, Nos D1100–D1111 and D1500–D1900 (TOPS Nos, various in 47001–47901 series)

These machines were powered by Sulzer 12-cylinder, twin-banked engines rated at 2,750hp when new, and offered a maximum speed of 95mph. The electrical engineer had lightened the equipment and reduced the locomotive's weight to approximately the equivalent of a diesel-hydraulic and for a cheaper outlay because hydraulic transmission was restricted to a maximum output of about 2,000hp. Above that figure, two engines and transmissions were required, whereas a diesel-electric could have one large engine and a generator.

Most of the first 300 locomotives had steam train heating boilers initially, but these were later removed or isolated and in many cases this was replaced or supplemented by electric train supply (ETS). Some later ones were equipped for electric train heating at 850V from new and with alternators providing an auxiliary 110V supply. The long life of many of these locomotives, with several still in main line operation today, has seen numerous alterations to equipment, including re-engining of some (reclassified as Class 57) and in consequence, much renumbering in the 47xxx series.

The class was distributed rapidly over the Western Region, but then in 1964 had to be withdrawn for modification to the Sulzer engines. With hiccups ironed out, they proved to be useful, economical and long-lived locomotives. At home equally on passenger and freight duties they were capable of restarting a load of 1,600 tons on a 1-in-100 gradient – a task which would have required two steam locomotives.

↑ No. D1522 at Mangotsfield, in original two-tone green livery, but with yellow warning panel, heads a Bristol to Newcastle express on 25 October 1966. The South West to North East trains ceased travelling via Mangotsfield on 3 January 1970. The lines to Bath in the foreground still show signs of occasional use at this time. *(Rev. Alan Newman)*

◩ No. D1538 at King's Cross on 28 May 1968. On the left is the well-known Gasworks Tunnel. *(Rev. Alan Newman)*

◩ Puffing out exhaust, blue-liveried No. 1585 leaves Bradford-on-Avon with a down passenger train on 6 June 1973. *(Rev. Alan Newman)*

⬆ No. 1592, in two-tone green and full-yellow ends, heads the down 'Devonian' at Bleadon & Uphill on 4 June 1971. The train describer, unusually, comprises pieces of printed paper stuck on the outside of the indicator panel. The telegraph posts carry an impressive number of wires. *(Rev. Alan Newman)*

⬆ No. 1598 at Paddington Platform 4 on 17 May 1971. The driver seems to have a problem in seeing as he is peering into the sun through a grimy windscreen. *(Rev. Alan Newman)*

⬈ No. D1599 leaves Westbury on 26 July 1968 with an extraordinarily short train to Bristol Temple Meads. *(Rev. Alan Newman)*

➡ No. D1606 and 'Western' class diesel-hydraulic No. D1067 *Western Druid* make an unusual pairing as they approach Bath with the 08.45 Paddington to Bristol Temple Meads on 10 June 1968. *(Rev. Alan Newman)*

▣ No. D1613 crosses the 77yd-long Bradford Viaduct just west of Bradford-on-Avon station on 26 May 1967. On the left can be seen some Second World War concrete tank traps. *(Rev. Alan Newman)*

◁ No. 1653 runs through Charfield hauling ex-Somerset & Dorset Class 7F No. 53808 en route from Barry scrapyard to Bristol via Gloucester on 3 October 1970, the 2-8-0 having been secured for preservation. Dead steam engines were prohibited from passing through the Severn Tunnel, as extra safety precautions were taken for traffic on this route. For instance, inspectors at Pilning and Severn Tunnel Junction checked every freight train going through the tunnel to ensure that loads in open wagons were secure. If there was any doubt about a wagon it was removed from the train and sent via Gloucester, as a derailment in the tunnel would have been a serious problem. Charfield brickworks can be seen in the background. *(Rev. Alan Newman)*

▲ No. 1662 *Isambard Kingdom Brunel* near Knighton Crossing, with a down express on 7 October 1971. This was one of the relatively few members of the class given a name in BR days. *(Rev. Alan Newman)*

⬆ No. D1674 passes Bradford-on-Avon goods shed with an up freight in June 1967. The adjacent goods yard has its track lifted but the loading gauge is still in position at the end of the goods shed. The cattle dock is relatively weed-free. *(Rev. Alan Newman)*

↗ No. D1723 is about to cross the river at Bradford-on-Avon on 16 May 1966, running light. The livery of the engine blends in well with the background. The platelayers' cabin to the right of the locomotive is almost overgrown with vegetation. *(Rev. Alan Newman)*

➡ No. D1724 heads down coal empties west of Bradford-on-Avon on 5 April 1968. The bottom-door discharge hopper wagons are lettered 'House Coal Concentration'. *(Rev. Alan Newman)*

No. 1726 is viewed from the cab of No. 1668 at Westbury on 26 July 1973 as it heads a train of Amalgamated Roadstone hopper wagons. *(Rev. Alan Newman)*

No. D1757 is seen west of Bradford-on-Avon with a train of open wagons on 7 November 1967. *(Rev. Alan Newman)*

No. D1764 heads a down local passenger train of suburban stock on the ECML at Hadley Wood on 14 October 1968. *(Rev. Alan Newman)*

⬆ No. 1766 passes the large signalbox at King's Cross station on 4 April 1970. *(Rev. Alan Newman)*

↗ No. 47091 *Thor*, another of the Western Region named locomotives, enters Bath Spa with the ten-coach 14.17 Southampton to Cardiff working on 22 June 1974. Formerly No. 1677 it retains its steam heating boiler, and under TOPS is classified Class 47/0. This engine had taken over the train at Salisbury. *(Rev. Alan Newman)*

➡ No. 47345 resides at Bristol Bath Road on 4 March 1977, its BR blue paintwork looking rather neglected. Formerly No. 1826, under TOPS it is a Class 47/3, the grouping for locomotives built without train heating equipment, primarily for freight duties. Locomotives in the background include a Class 37, three 350hp diesel shunters and a Class 50. *(Rev. Alan Newman)*

No. D1851 passes over Dillicar Troughs near Tebay with an up Freightliner train on 15 June 1967. (*Rev. Alan Newman*)

No. D1902 works through Little Somerford with a down freight on 8 August 1966. The station was formerly the junction with the Malmesbury branch, which closed to passengers on 8 September 1951 and freight on 11 November 1962. The platform roads are out of use and are being lifted. The barrow crossing is still in place, as is the small goods shed, and a water crane stands between the up platform road and the through road. (*Rev. Alan Newman*)

No. D1917 hauls a down freight through Bradford-on-Avon on 11 October 1966. (*Rev. Alan Newman*)

⬆ No. 1918 emits a plume of exhaust as it powers an up coal train at Chipping Sodbury on 2 October 1971. An aqueduct carrying a stream across the line can be seen towards the rear of the train. *(Rev. Alan Newman)*

↗ On the up loop line, No. 1924 approaches Pilning from the Severn Tunnel with a coal train on a frosty 15 February 1971. Such loops permitted faster trains to overtake slow goods. The 97yd-long Ableton Lane Tunnel is in the distance. *(Rev. Alan Newman)*

➡ Nos 1925 and 1552 offer a contrast in liveries at Bristol Bath Road depot on 24 May 1973. *(Rev. Alan Newman)*

⬆ No. 1928 leaves Bradford-on-Avon with a Portsmouth to Bristol train on 14 November 1972. *(Rev. Alan Newman)*

➡ No. D1933 poses at Bristol Bath Road depot on 30 April 1966 clearly showing the Brush builder's plate (No. 695 of 1966). The photographer's son, Francis, leans from the cab. *(Rev. Alan Newman)*

No. D1983 heads a down train at Hadley Wood Tunnel, comprising a rake of maroon and blue/grey-liveried coaches, on 14 October 1968. (*Rev. Alan Newman*)

No. D1998 undergoing a steam boiler test at Crewe Works on 8 June 1966. The boiler was required for steam heating the coaches. (*Rev. Alan Newman*)

⬆ No. 6752 leaves Liverpool Street with the morning 'Hook Continental' to Harwich Parkestone Quay for the ferry to the Hook of Holland on 12 October 1970. *(Rev. Alan Newman)*

Class 37
English Electric Type 3 Co-Co diesel-electric

309 built, introduced 1960–5
Nos D6600–D6608 and D6700–D6999
(Initial TOPS Nos 37001–37308)

The English Electric 12-cylinder 1,750hp engine fitted to the Type 3 offered a maximum speed of 80mph; the locomotive weighed 108 tons and was comparable with a 'Hymek' 1,700hp diesel-hydraulic. Classified as Class 37 under TOPS, these multi-purpose locomotives had the advantages of better availability, and a lower initial cost and casualty rate and they became BR's standard Type 3 power. The 'nose' extension in front of the cab houses traction motor blowers, a compressor and exhausters.

In the summer of 1966, Nos D6875–D6895 were re-geared for 100mph running and, operating in pairs, worked Western Region expresses such as Paddington to Bristol or South Wales. However, they proved technically unsuitable for this duty and within months their rosters were handled by 90mph 'Westerns'. The Class 37 has been one of BR's most successful types, seeing widespread operation, with several examples still at work on the main line today as well as many in use on heritage railways.

⬆ No. D6802 looking resplendent at NCB Cortonwood Colliery sidings, South Yorkshire, on 10 September 1968. It was the announcement of the closure of this pit that ignited the miners' strike of 1984, the miners here being the first to down tools. The site is now occupied by a retail park. *(Rev. Alan Newman)*

↗ Nos D6881 and D6882 are seen at Bristol Temple Meads on 1 June 1966. No. D6881 is being towed dead and carries an oil tail lamp, perhaps because its electrics are inoperative. *(Rev. Alan Newman)*

➡ Nos D6892 and D6877 approach Bath Spa with a down express on 6 May 1966. The signal is for the up bay platform, which was taken out of use on 31 March 1967, and Bath Spa signalbox closed on 21 January 1968. *(Rev. Alan Newman)*

◄ Nos 6921 and 6993 at Pilning on 14 September 1970 with an Aberthaw Power Station to Puxton pulverised fly ash train. Puxton, west of Bristol, was the railhead used for the M5 motorway construction. Ableton Lane Tunnel is in the background. *(Rev. Alan Newman)*

◣ No. D6925 runs light down Upton Scudamore Bank after delivering a banana train to Warminster on 2 September 1967. The concrete fence posts, probably cast at Taunton, are new. *(Rev. Alan Newman)*

◢ Quite an extensive variety of locomotives is on display at Liverpool Street on 12 October 1970. From right to left: English Electric Type 3 No. 6960, Brush Type 4 No. 1528, Brush Type 2 No. 5532, BTH Type 1 No. 8234, and EE Type 3 No. 6727. *(Rev. Alan Newman)*

◄ Nos 6981 and 6875 arrive at Puxton from Aberthaw Power Station on 20 April 1970 with pulverised fly ash for M5 construction. The site of the former creamery siding can be seen on the right. The cloud of dust to the left of the train is presumably fly ash flying. *(Rev. Alan Newman)*

▲ Nos 6981 and 6875 set back into the siding at Puxton with the fly ash train, on 20 April 1970. *(Rev. Alan Newman)*

⬆ Following the introduction of TOPS, the EE Type 3s became Class 37. Here, No. 37292, formerly No. 6992, is seen at Bristol Bath Road depot on 4 March 1977. The signalbox, left, built when the station was modernised in the mid-1930s, governed the entrance to the locomotive depot. *(Rev. Alan Newman)*

➡ No. 37159, formerly No. 6859, passes Staverton, Wiltshire, with empty tank wagons from Melksham for the oil installation at Llandarcy, on 29 November 1978. The track had been singled from 26 February 1967. *(Rev. Alan Newman)*

Class 33 Birmingham Railway Carriage & Wagon Company Type 3 Bo-Bo diesel-electric

98 built, introduced 1960–2, Nos D6500–D6597 (Initial TOPS Nos 33001–33065, 33101–33119 and 33201–33212)

These very successful locomotives were powered by a Sulzer eight-cylinder 1,550hp engine, which was an enlarged version of the six-cylinder Sulzer engine used in the earlier Class 24. The Birmingham Type 3 had a maximum speed of 85mph and a weight of only 78 tons. They were equipped with a generator for electric train heating.

The class was based entirely on the Southern Region, especially on lines of the former London, Brighton & South Coast Railway and the South Eastern & Chatham Railway initially. They were used for freight and certain Kent Coast trains which were not emu worked. With the extension of the third rail to Bournemouth in 1967, the imaginative plan was adopted of adapting Class 33 locomotives for push-pull working. On arrival at Bournemouth of a train from Waterloo, the locomotive would back on to the leading coach of a trailer set forming the front portion of the emu and haul this unit to Weymouth, thus obviating any need for passengers to change trains. On the return, the 'Crompton', as they were nicknamed due to their Crompton Parkinson electrical equipment, would leave Weymouth propelling the coaches to Bournemouth where they would be coupled to the rear of an emu for the rest of the journey to Waterloo.

Locomotives modified for this service were classified Class 33/1. They had the advantage that their remote-control equipment also allowed them to work in multiple with emus or electro-diesel locomotives.

Another variation, later classified TOPS Class 33/2, was built with narrower bodies for use on the restricted-clearance Tonbridge to Hastings line. From October 1971, Class 33s replaced 'Warships' on Waterloo to Exeter trains until they were ousted by the Class 50s in 1980. A good number survive in preservation, as well as a few passed for main line operation.

↑ No. D6503 waits beneath an impressive array of signals at Bournemouth Central on 25 June 1966, with Ivatt Class 2 2-6-2T No. 41224 in the foreground. It makes an interesting comparison in the shape and livery of the two forms of motive power, and it is a matter of opinion as to which is the more pleasing. *(Rev. Alan Newman)*

Clean-looking No. 6515 enters Salisbury with a down goods on 15 May 1973. This locomotive has survived into preservation and recently underwent a major overhaul in Eastleigh Works, just as it would have done when in BR ownership. *(Rev. Alan Newman)*

Nos D6500 and D6545 head a down freight at Salisbury on 20 May 1966. The dummy signal on the ground is in the 'off' position. *(Rev. Alan Newman)*

Nos 6514 and 6543 travel as up light engines at Clink Road Junction, Frome, on 27 February 1973. The signalbox was brought into use on 18 December 1932, but was then switched out, it being reopened together with the new Frome avoiding line on 2 January 1933. The gas cylinders by the base of the box may have been provided for cooking facilities. Notice the scorched grass by the timber signalbox, which finally closed on 6 October 1984. The overbridge is a typical Wilts, Somerset & Weymouth Railway structure. *(Rev. Alan Newman)*

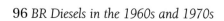

96 BR Diesels in the 1960s and 1970s

↖ A Waterloo to Exeter train leaves Salisbury on 13 July 1972 behind No. 6527 emitting a cloud of fumes. Class 08 diesel shunter No. D3274 is on the left. The 'Crompton' is now preserved on the Bodmin & Wenford Railway and carries its later TOPS Class 33/1 number, 33110. *(Rev. Alan Newman)*

← No. D6529 is seen at Westbury with a train of Woking to Frome ballast empties on 30 July 1968. The area to the right of the locomotive is now the site of the MAS signalbox which opened on 13 May 1984. *(Rev. Alan Newman)*

↑ No. D6531 passes Westbury signalbox after having arrived with a Woking to Frome empty ballast train on 26 September 1968. The box closed on 27 April 1984. *(Rev. Alan Newman)*

98 BR Diesels in the 1960s and 1970s

▣ No. 6534 arrives at Salisbury with an up parcels train on
13 July 1972. It is fitted with a small snow plough. Salisbury West
signal box can be seen to the left of the train. The track layout
today is a shadow of its former self. *(Rev. Alan Newman)*

◀ No. 6541 propels a loaded ballast train out of the north end
of Westbury station on 3 April 1969, past a splendid array of
signals. *(Rev. Alan Newman)*

▲ No. 6551 in almost pristine condition hauls a down train at
Salisbury on 13 July 1972. The first five vehicles are permanent
way wagons and the remainder are goods stock. The Type 3 is
fitted with a snow plough, all members of the class being fitted
with snow plough brackets. *(Rev. Alan Newman)*

⬆ No. D6553 in green livery with yellow ends, working a Frome to Woking ballast train, climbs the 1-in-70 Upton Scudamore Bank on 26 July 1968. This engine, TOPS No. 33035, has survived and is privately owned and kept at Barrow Hill roundhouse. *(Rev. Alan Newman)*

↗ No. D6578 passes Fairwood Junction, Westbury, with an up ballast train on 17 February 1969, taking the line through Westbury station, rather than the cut-off route. In line with the front of the locomotive can be seen the 'T' board indicating the termination of a speed restriction, meaning that normal line speed can be resumed. *(Rev. Alan Newman)*

➡ Nos D6585 and D6541 rest at Eastleigh depot on 25 April 1966. They are in original BR green livery with cream lining and not yet adorned with yellow warning panels. The ballast is ash from steam locomotives which, as from the following year, was to become a thing of the past. *(Rev. Alan Newman)*

⬅ Class 33/0 No. 33017, previously No. 6526, leaves Trowbridge with up stone empties on 6 June 1974. A brake van is placed midway along the train. *(Rev. Alan Newman)*

⬆ No. 33117, previously No. 6536, waits at Weymouth Quay with a boat train to Waterloo on 31 August 1974. Notice the brightly polished bell and hazard light set above the buffer beam. The cables on either side indicate that the locomotive is fitted for push-pull working with multiple unit stock and is thus classified as Class 33/1. It is now based on the East Lancashire Railway. On the left is an oil tank wagon for refuelling the Channel Islands ferries. *(Rev. Alan Newman)*

⬆ An unidentified 'Hymek' in original green livery, works a two non-corridor
coach stopping train from Bristol Temple Meads to Severn Beach at Sneyd
Park c1961. *(Author's collection)*

Class 35 Beyer Peacock Type 3 'Hymek' B-B diesel-hydraulic

101 built, introduced 1961–4, Nos D7000–D7100

The 'Hymek' name comes from an amalgam of the hydraulic Mekydro transmission, fitted to these locomotives, which were powered by 1,700hp Maybach engines. They weighed 77 tons and had a maximum speed of 90mph. Equipped with steam heating they were comparable with the Birmingham RCW Type 3 (Class 33) diesel-electrics. A report published in 1965 revealed that the EE Type 3 (Class 37) had an advantage over the 'Hymeks' in availability, first cost, and casualties.

Arguably, the 'Hymeks' were the most attractive-looking of the BR's diesel locomotives. They covered a range of duties from the lighter expresses to freight working and banking, either singly or in multiple, including up the 1-in-37.7 Lickey incline. Locomotives on this duty had the first stage of their Mekydro transmission locked out to avoid a gear change and thus experience a temporary loss of power, perhaps just when it was most needed. The last of the class was withdrawn in 1975 with four examples surviving in preservation.

No. 7001 passes Fairwood Junction signalbox, Westbury, with the 09.41 Weymouth to Westbury service on 22 February 1971. Despite the winter date, the sun shining into the box obviously makes it feel hot as the signalman has a window open. *(Rev. Alan Newman)*

No. D7002 in green livery is seen at Westbury with the 09.35 Cardiff to Portsmouth train on 19 February 1970. A wagon of scrap is just visible on the far right. *(Rev. Alan Newman)*

No. D7003 passes Clink Road Junction, Frome, with a down goods on 5 November 1970. *(Rev. Alan Newman)*

⬆ No. D7003 again, but heading the 14.23 Portsmouth to Bristol passenger train, comprising SR stock in green livery. It emerges into the sunlight from the ornate portal of Twerton Tunnel, between Bath and Bristol, on 13 July 1963. *(Author)*

↗ No. D7007 at Freshford with the 13.30 Saturdays-only Bournemouth to Cardiff on 29 August 1970. Although in blue livery it still carries the 'D' prefix to its number. The numerals were cast metal and only some examples had the 'D' removed, with none ever receiving their TOPS 35xxx numbers. The driver and second man can be seen in the cab. *(Rev. Alan Newman)*

➡ No. D7010 negotiates Clink Road Junction, Frome, on 25 September 1970, working the 09.30 Weymouth to Westbury service. Much paint has peeled from the roof of the first coach leaving the steel exposed. *(Rev. Alan Newman)*

⬆ Blue-liveried No. D7012 runs through at Bradford-on-Avon on 11 April 1968 with a down train of 'Presflo' cement wagons. *(Rev. Alan Newman)*

⬇ No. D7013 in green livery with small yellow warning panels, departs from Bradford-on-Avon with a Portsmouth to Cardiff working on 14 February 1970. A light fall of snow is in evidence. *(Rev. Alan Newman)*

⬆ No. D7017 poses at Bath goods depot on 14 April 1967. Although the livery is several years old, the paintwork has been kept clean, with the addition of a yellow warning panel. Notwithstanding that quite a lot of track has been lifted, the Midland Bridge Road goods depot remained open until 31 May 1971. No. D7017 is maintained in operational condition on the West Somerset Railway and has been returned to this livery. The railway is also home to sister loco No. D7018, undergoing a long-term overhaul. *(Rev. Alan Newman)*

⬇ Restored to its original two-tone green livery, No. D7017 is shown as preserved on the West Somerset Railway at Minehead on 20 August 1979. Between the vans and coaches can be seen ex-LBSCR 'Terrier' 0-6-0T No. 32678 formerly at Butlin's holiday camp. *(Rev. Alan Newman)*

◩ No. D7017 again, but in trouble, with its leading bogie derailed at Shirehampton in 1961. The brake van leans at a precarious angle. Shirehampton goods yard was kept open for coal until the 1980s, the line having been singled from 19 October 1970. *(Author's collection)*

◁ On the right is No. D7022 at Bristol Bath Road on 1 June 1966. Beyond this can be seen Brush Type 4 No. D1720, 'Western' No. D1013 *Western Ranger*, BR Type 1 diesel-hydraulic No. D9521, and an EE Type 3. *(Rev. Alan Newman)*

◪ No. 7022 stands at Cranmore with bitumen tank wagons on 21 October 1974. Bitumen was loaded into road tankers for onwards transit to local quarries for making Tarmac. The rail tanks were heated by gas burners to ease the flow for unloading. The last tanker train on this line ran in September 1985, following which the station and sidings were taken over by the East Somerset Railway. *(Rev. Alan Newman)*

↑ No. D7025 gleaming in the sunshine, passes Bradford-on-Avon with a train comprising vans and 'Presflos' on 4 April 1967. *(Rev. Alan Newman)*

↗ No. D7031 is seen on the Somerset & Dorset line with two brake vans near Moorewood Sidings, between Chilcompton and Binegar, on 8 March 1968. It is proceeding to pick up lifted track on bogie bolsters, the S&D having closed two years earlier, on 7 March 1966. The concrete blocks in the foreground were to deter invading tanks during the Second World War. *(Rev. Alan Newman)*

➡ No. D7031 is seen again, this time east of Warminster with a Cardiff to Portsmouth train on 17 February 1969. The overbridge in the distance, left, is of typical Wilts, Somerset & Weymouth Railway design. *(Rev. Alan Newman)*

◤ No. D7033 enters ARC's Hapsford Quarry Sidings near Frome on 8 March 1968 with side-tipping ballast wagons. *(Rev. Alan Newman)*

◀ On 8 March 1968, No. D7033 has uncoupled from its train of empty wagons, run round and stands by No. 1, a four-wheeled vertical boiler Sentinel (9374 of 1947). *(Rev. Alan Newman)*

↑ No. D7038 runs light engine west of Bradford-on-Avon on 8 April 1968. *(Rev. Alan Newman)*

⬆ No. 7039 waits at Trowbridge with the Saturdays-only 12.45 Cardiff to Westbury service on 4 May 1972. The bay platform line on the left has been lifted. In 1984, the Brunel-style buildings were declared unsafe, demolished and a modern replacement erected. The footbridge was replaced and the one seen here is now awaiting re-erection at Williton on the West Somerset Railway. *(Rev. Alan Newman)*

⬇ No. D7040 passes Fairwood Junction, Westbury, with an up mixed freight on 17 February 1969 and is taking the line through Westbury station. Some re-ballasting has taken place recently and the signalman has a fire burning. *(Rev. Alan Newman)*

⬆ No. D7041 with the 09.20 Portsmouth to Bristol Temple Meads, crosses the weir as it departs from Bradford-on-Avon on 19 February 1971. *(Rev. Alan Newman)*

⬇ Nos D7042 and D7039, running light at Westbury on 5 April 1969, make an interesting contrast in liveries. *(Rev. Alan Newman)*

No. D7043 passes Clink Road Junction, Frome, with an up stone train from Hapsford Quarry on 25 September 1970. The front wagons are all of the bottom-door discharge type. *(Rev. Alan Newman)*

No. D7045 waits for the road at Hawkeridge Junction, Westbury, on 29 March 1967. It stands on the double-track loop opened on 14 July 1942 to enable trains to run from the Newbury direction to Trowbridge, which was useful for wartime traffic and diversions. Hawkeridge signalbox opened with the loop and closed in May 1984. *(Rev. Alan Newman)*

No. D7047 stands on the turntable at Bristol Bath Road on 22 October 1966. Although diesel locomotives did not generally need turning, the facility was useful if one suffered something such as a cracked windscreen. *(Author)*

'Hymek' reflection: No. 7050 leaves Bradford-on-Avon on 26 September 1972 with the 09.52 Weymouth to Bristol Temple Meads. *(Rev. Alan Newman)*

No. D7055 is seen at Avoncliff with a Cardiff to Portsmouth train on 5 May 1970. A permanent way hut stands on the left. *(Rev. Alan Newman)*

↑ No. D7058 in deplorable external condition with blistered paintwork, passes Chipping Sodbury with a South Wales to Paddington express on 2 October 1971. An aqueduct spans the track towards the rear of the train. *(Rev. Alan Newman)*

↗ No. D7060, in charge of a mixed freight, crosses the 77yd-long Bradford Viaduct on 27 January 1969. *(Rev. Alan Newman)*

→ No. 7068 heads a Portsmouth to Bristol train away from Bradford-on-Avon station on 15 November 1972, its paintwork not exactly in pristine condition. The four-character headcode panel displays '2V60'. The first character is the class of train; the 'V' denotes it is inter-regional, and the third and fourth enable a signalman to determine its identity for reporting purposes. *(Rev. Alan Newman)*

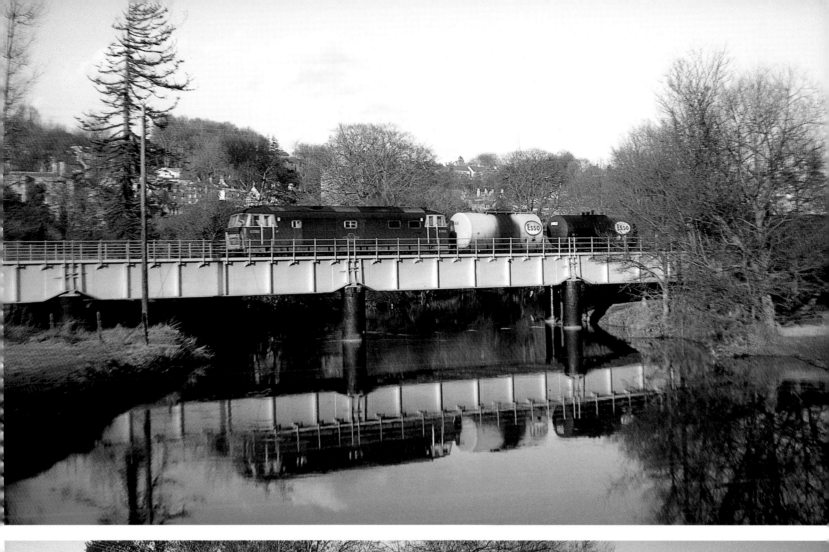

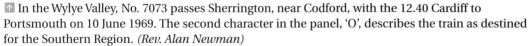 In the Wylye Valley, No. 7073 passes Sherrington, near Codford, with the 12.40 Cardiff to Portsmouth on 10 June 1969. The second character in the panel, 'O', describes the train as destined for the Southern Region. *(Rev. Alan Newman)*

↗ No. 7076 negotiates Clink Road Junction, Frome, with empty bitumen tank wagons from Cranmore on 27 February 1970. This engine has survived into preservation and is based on the East Lancashire Railway. *(Rev. Alan Newman)*

➡ No. 7080 leaves Bradford-on-Avon with the 09.52 Weymouth to Bristol Temple Meads service on 26 June 1972. *(Rev. Alan Newman)*

→ No. D7090 passes Avoncliff Halt with a down mixed freight on 5 January 1967. This halt opened on 9 July 1906 and is still open to passengers today, due to road access in the area being difficult because of the steep, winding lanes which are quite unsuitable for buses. (Rev. Alan Newman)

← No. D7091 approaches Heywood Junction, Westbury, with a down passenger train on 29 July 1966. The tail traffic consists of a four-wheeled van and two bogie vans.
(Rev. Alan Newman)

⬆ Class 31 No. 5539 on a test and crew training run from Old Oak Common to Westbury on 5 April 1969. The locomotive and first two coaches look immaculate. *(Rev. Alan Newman)*

Class 31 Brush Type 2 A1A-A1A diesel-electric

263 built, introduced 1957–62, Nos D5500–D5699 and D5800–D5862 (Initial TOPS Nos 31001–31019; 31101–31327 and 31400–31417)

Originally built with Mirrlees 1,250hp, 1,365hp, or 1,600hp engines, all were re-equipped from 1964 with English Electric 1,470hp units, being reclassified under TOPS from Class 30 to 31. The weight of the re-engined locomotives was 107–113 tons. Some bogies and underframes were built by Beyer Peacock and others by W. G. Bagnall, better known for industrial locomotives. The locomotives were erected at Brush Electrical Engineering Co. Ltd, Falcon Works at Loughborough. The non-powered centre wheels were of 3ft 3½in diameter compared with the outer, powered wheels of 3ft 7in.

When new, all were delivered to the Eastern Region, but with the demise of the hydraulics a number were transferred to the Western Region. Initially used on empty coaching stock working at Paddington, they later also appeared on express duties such as Paddington to Birmingham or Worcester. Later, some found their way to the London Midland Region. The class was the last survivor in the United Kingdom of the A1A-A1A wheel arrangement and several are now preserved on heritage railways, while a few are still at work on the national system including those used by Network Rail.

No. D5589 was delivered new to Eastern Region 34B Hornsey depot in February 1960 and is seen in original green livery with the addition of yellow ends, at King's Cross on 1 June 1967. It was later renumbered 31401. *(Rev. Alan Newman)*

No. 5623 has just passed through Hadley Wood Tunnel on 14 October 1968 with a train of empty wagons. In the days before all vehicles were fitted with automatic brakes, a brake van had to be placed at the rear of the train. *(Rev. Alan Newman)*

No. D5645 is seen at Hadley Wood on 13 October 1969 with a rake of non-corridor coaches wearing a variety of liveries. *(Rev. Alan Newman)*

◤ No. D5649 in later BR Rail blue with yellow ends, at King's Cross on 1 June 1967, the loco crew looking towards the rear suggesting it is setting back. It was later renumbered under TOPS as 31223.
(*Rev. Alan Newman*)

◄ No. 5827 with the Bristol–Salisbury parcels train unusually taking the Melksham line at Bradford Junctions on 5 September 1973.
(*Rev. Alan Newman*)

◤ No. 5828, soon to be renumbered 31295, heads a mixed train including tank wagons, west of Bradford-on-Avon on 25 April 1973.
(*Rev. Alan Newman*)

⬆ Class 31/1 No. 31295 (previously No. 5828) fitted with dual (BR and WR) AWS (automatic warning system), approaches Bradford-on-Avon with a Bristol to Salisbury parcels train on 25 January 1974. The first vehicle is an ex-SR PMV (parcels and miscellaneous van) followed by CCTs (covered carriage trucks). *(Rev. Alan Newman)*

↗ Class 31/1 No. 31309 (ex-5843) fitted with dual AWS, works the 10.05 Weymouth to Bristol Temple Meads train, leaving Bradford-on-Avon on 25 January 1974. *(Rev. Alan Newman)*

➡ Diesel parade at York on 5 July 1979: Class 31/4 No. 31417 fitted with electric train heating equipment; Class 25/2 No. 25088 with modified cab details and GEC Series 2 equipment; and Class 31/1s Nos 31204 and 31247. *(Rev. Alan Newman)*

Class 24 and 25 BR Type 2 Bo-Bo diesel-electrics

151 Class 24 built, introduced 1958–61,
Nos D5000–D5150 (TOPS Nos 24001–24150)
327 Class 25 built, introduced 1961-67,
Nos D5151–D5299 and D7500–D7677
(TOPS Nos 25001–25327)

The first 151 locomotives were built by BR at their Crewe, Derby and Darlington works and were fitted with 1,160hp six-cylinder Sulzer engines giving a maximum speed of 75mph. The remaining locomotives, later Class 25, had 1,250hp Sulzer engines and were constructed at BR Darlington and Derby works as well as a batch by Beyer Peacock. The two similar-looking classes were used throughout the BR network at various times, including 24s on the Southern Region for a short period prior to the Kent Coast electrification, and 25s going to the Western Region in early 1972 to replace 'Hymeks'. Several examples of each class are to be found at work on heritage railways today.

⬆ Class 24 No. 5079 waits at Aberystwyth station on 4 June 1970, the train comprising two parcels vans and three coaches.
(Rev. Alan Newman)

⬆ Class 24s Nos D5110 and D5107 are seen at Tyne Dock with an iron-ore train on 14 June 1967. *(Rev. Alan Newman)*

⬇ Class 25s Nos 7519 and 5182 run through Severn Tunnel Junction as light engines on 4 September 1972. Unlike the earlier locomotives which had nose-end doors, No. 7519 has a plain front end. On the left stands the Severn Tunnel firefighting train equipped with water tanks. *(Rev. Alan Newman)*

⬆ Work-stained Class 25s Nos D7528 and D7631 stand outside the traction maintenance depot at Leicester on 26 February 1968. *(Rev. Alan Newman)*

⬇ Class 25 No. D7660 trundles past Leicester traction maintenance depot on 26 February 1968. *(Rev. Alan Newman)*

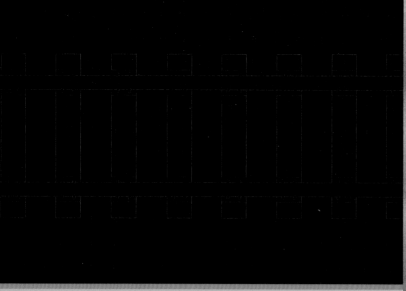

Classes 26 and 27 Birmingham Railway Carriage & Wagon Company Type 2 Bo-Bo diesel-electrics

47 Class 26 built, introduced 1958–9,
Nos D5300–D5346 (TOPS Nos 26001–26046)
69 Class 27 built, introduced 1961–2,
Nos D5347–D5415 (TOPS Nos 27001–27044
and 27101–27124)

These 116 locomotives were all constructed at the BRCW's works in Smethwick, the first 47 having 1,160hp Sulzer engines and the others 1,250hp units. Initial deliveries were to the Eastern, Scottish, North Eastern and London Midland regions, but all were eventually based in Scotland. There are 13 Class 26s and eight Class 27s surviving in preservation.

⬆ An unidentified BRCW Type 2 rests at Fort William in August 1963 with another of the same class in the distance, on a different road, with a 350hp shunter alongside. *(R.E. Toop)*

◥ Class 26 No. D5322 passes an up goods train at Stromeferry in charge of a down goods, on 31 August 1962. The footbridge is worthy of note and the left-hand platform has been extended at a standard height. In the station yard is a Standard Vanguard car. *(Author)*

◀ Later the same day, No. D5322 is seen again but on a more prestigious duty, with an observation coach at the Kyle of Lochalsh. This Pullman car originally ran between Waterloo and Ilfracombe on the 'Devon Belle'. Behind the coaches to the left are extensive cattle pens. *(Author)*

⬆ Class 27 No. D5410 heads an Oban to Glasgow train near Connel Ferry in August 1968. This engine is now preserved on the Severn Valley Railway. The bridge beyond the Type 2 carried the Ballachulish branch. *(R.E. Toop)*

Type 2 North British Type 2 B-B Diesel-hydraulic

58 built, introduced 1959–62, Nos D6300–D6357

For use on BR Western Region, North British supplied these locomotives, which were similar to the company's previous (TOPS Class 21) locomotives numbered D6100–D6157, but were equipped with hydraulic rather than electric transmission. The first six hydraulics had 1,000hp MAN engines, but the later examples had the benefit of another 100hp. Both classes proved to be very short lived, with no survivors.

No. 6308 is seen at Marsh Junction, Bristol, on 29 October 1971, heading a line of sister engines that had been withdrawn from service in the previous month. *(Rev. Alan Newman)*

No. D6321 works a track-lifting train on the former Somerset & Dorset line at Wellow on 2 November 1967. *(Author)*

Diesel Shunters

Class 14 BR Type 1 0-6-0 diesel-hydraulic

56 built, introduced 1964–5, Nos D9500–D9555

Powered by a Paxman 650hp Ventura engine, these locomotives were built at Swindon Works for the Western Region. Maximum speed was 40mph and its weight 51 tons. They were designed for shunting and trip working where a higher speed was required than was available from a Class 08 diesel-electric. However, the class appeared too late on the scene as by the time they entered service, freight rationalisation had rendered them redundant before turning a wheel. By late 1966, 20 had been placed in store and most were withdrawn during 1968 with just a few left in traffic until 26 April 1969. The design proved to be a success in the long term however, as many had a second career in industry, both at home and abroad. Several are still in operation today on heritage railways and on contract hire.

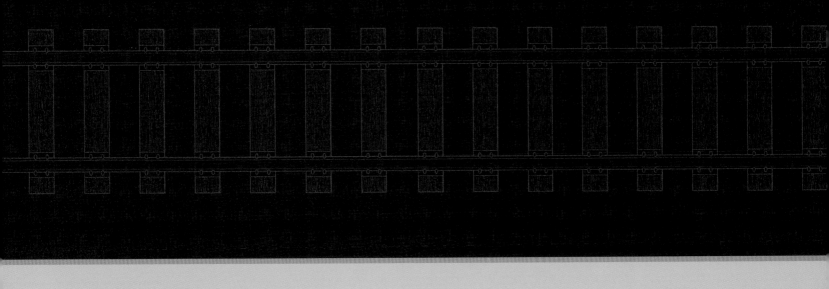

Class 08 BR 0-6-0 diesel-electric shunter

This English Electric 350hp design dates back to the 1930s and particularly to the 1945 LMS model and was built in large quantities, with numerous detail variations. The two axle-hung traction motors were capable of a maximum speed of 20mph. The locomotive weighed 50 tons. It was the first diesel-electric engine built for BR in quantity and was superior to steam for shunting duties as it was unnecessary to return to the shed daily for water, coal and fire-cleaning.

The controller is coupled mechanically to the engine governor. Early notches cut out resistance by steps and so increase generator excitation, while a further movement of the controller increases engine speed up to the maximum.

With hindsight, too many of the class were built in view of the closing of goods yards and branch lines, coupled with a general fall of truckload, as opposed to trainload traffic. Certainly, it is the opinion of some commentators that in some cases it would have been more economic to have retained steam shunting engines a little longer, until the traffic declined. Many examples are still found at work on the national network, in industry, and on heritage railways.

← The Class 14 'Teddy Bears', as they were often nicknamed, are represented here by No. D9523 (82A, Bristol, Bath Road shed plate on side of buffer beam) at Bath Green Park mpd on 18 March 1966. This was just 11 days after the withdrawal of steam in the area. The water softener can be seen beyond, as can part of a sludge tender to the left. No. D9523 has survived into preservation and is now on the Nene Valley Railway with other members of the class.
(*Rev. Alan Newman*)

→ Class 08 No. D3183 is seen at Radstock on 8 March 1968, its paintwork in poor condition.
(*Rev. Alan Newman*)

⬆ No. D3220 approaches the tunnel at Kemp Town on 12 August 1970. The 'XP' on the wagon, left, indicates it is fitted with vacuum brakes, has a wheelbase of not less than 10ft 6in, and was therefore suitable for running in passenger trains. *(Rev. Alan Newman)*

↗ No. D3272 is on shed at Eastleigh, 13 February 1967. The newly applied BR double-arrow emblem is above the number. *(Rev. Alan Newman)*

➡ With the reduction in the amount of shunting required, BR had surplus shunters. This locomotive, variously numbered 13044/D3044/08032, purchased by Foster Yeoman, became their No. 33 *Mendip* for use at that company's Merehead Stone Terminal, Somerset. It is viewed here on 3 June 1975. The history of 08s used at this busy location is long and complex with many examples having come and gone over the years. No. 08032 is currently on loan to the Mid-Hants Railway, but retains its Yeoman blue livery. *(Rev. Alan Newman)*

Class 07 Ruston & Hornsby 0-6-0 diesel-electric shunter

A total of 14 of these locomotives were bought in 1962 specifically to replace the USA class 0-6-0Ts at Southampton Docks. Weighing 42 tons 5cwt they had a 275hp Paxman six-cylinder engine driving through an AEI traction motor. A few survive in preservation, including No. D2995 illustrated here.

⬆ Class 07 No. D2995 works at Southampton Docks on 25 April 1966 on shunting duty No. 7. The shunter is riding towards the front on the far side of the locomotive. As so few were supplied to BR and they were withdrawn at a fairly early date, photographs of them working on BR are rare. *(Rev. Alan Newman)*

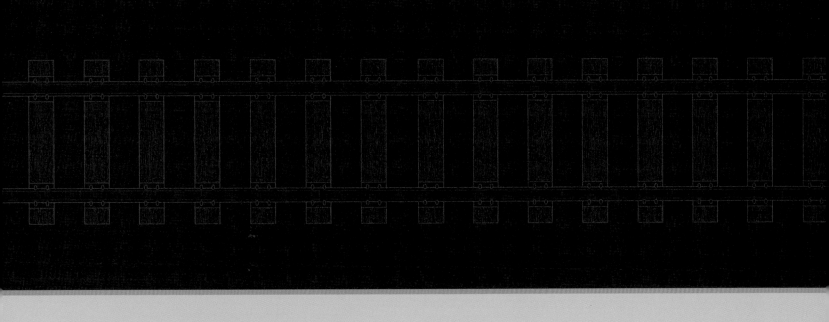

Class 03 BR 0-6-0 diesel mechanical shunter

These once widespread locomotives were powered by a Gardner 204hp engine driving through a five-speed epicyclic gearbox, offering a maximum speed of 28mph. They weighed 30 tons 16cwt. They appeared on all regions except the Scottish, but the duties for which they were designed quickly disappeared under rationalisation. Many then found a new lease of life in industry and, later, on heritage railways.

⬆ Class 03 No. 2009, acts as station pilot at Cambridge on 12 October 1970. The Cambridge-based yellow wagon is fitted with a vacuum brake which would give additional stopping power. Early members of this class, such as No. 2009, had a cone-shaped exhaust, while later examples had a chimney, reminiscent of a steam locomotive. *(Rev. Alan Newman)*

↖ No. D2187 pauses at Little Somerford on 15 June 1962 with the Swindon to Malmesbury goods train. It has the chimney-shaped exhaust. The brake van is a typical GWR 'Toad' design. *(Author)*

← No. D2187 forms part of the scene at Malmesbury on 15 June 1962. The station despatched large quantities of agricultural equipment manufactured by Alvan Blanch. The branch closed to passenger traffic on 10 September 1951 and to goods on 12 November 1962. Although the engine shed had closed in September 1951, it, the water tank and coaling stage, right, look in remarkably good condition. *(Author)*

↑ No. D2399, the last of its class, built at Doncaster in 1961, waits at Weymouth Quay on 22 July 1972. It carries a warning bell and behind it is a Stothert & Pitt dock crane built in Bath. The yellow Ford articulated unit, left, belongs to National Carriers Ltd, the firm which took over the road delivery and collection of parcels from BR. No. 2399 has survived into preservation at Mangapps Farm Railway, Essex. *(Rev. Alan Newman)*

Prototype locomotives

Class 53 Brush Type 4 Co-Co diesel-electric

Brush contract No. 280, Project Falcon, known as No. D0280 *Falcon*, was loaned to BR from October 1961. Fitted with two Maybach 1,440hp engines, transmission was by six Brush electric traction motors, and it weighed 115 tons. It was withdrawn in May 1974 and broken up at Newport in March 1976 as Brush would not allow BR to release it for preservation under the terms of their sales contract.

⬆ No. D0280 *Falcon* arrives at Bath Spa with the 07.20 Bristol Temple Meads to Paddington on 30 July 1968. The author was always pleased to see this one-off locomotive at the head of his train because he was assured of a punctual arrival at his destination. It was later bought by BR and given the number D1200. *(Author)*

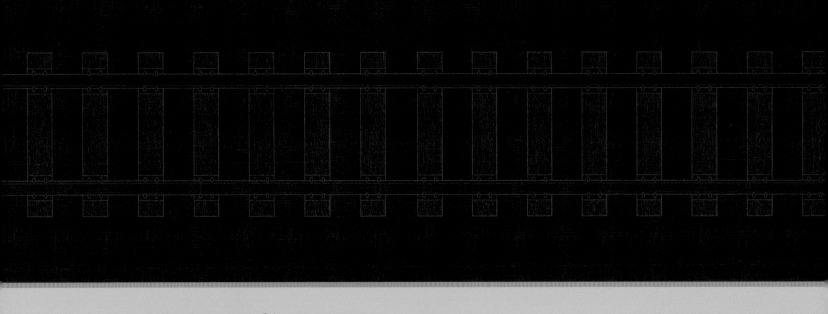

Brown-Boveri A1A-A1A gas turbine No. 18000

In the late 1940s, the LMS and SR planned diesel-electric locomotives, but in 1940, the GWR had ordered a gas turbine locomotive from Brown-Boveri. This was the third such locomotive in the world and following running trials in Switzerland, arrived in England in 1949, entering service on BR Western Region in May 1950. It worked express passenger trains between Paddington and Plymouth, and Paddington and Bristol, being restricted to the same routes as the 'Kings'. Following withdrawal in 1960 it returned to the manufacturers in Switzerland, but has since been brought back to England for preservation, and can currently be seen at Barrow Hill Roundhouse.

⬆ Prototype gas-turbine locomotive No. 18000 in green livery, as seen from a passing train, outside Swindon Works *c*1956.
(*J. A. Reid*)

Diesel railcars and multiple units

The 'Blue Pullman'

The 'Trans Europ Express' was launched on the Continent in 1957 and a dmu concept, known as the 'Blue Pullman', was seen as its British equivalent. The London Midland Region was allocated two six-car sets and the Western Region three eight-car trains. The LMR units were first class only, whereas the WR sets had some second-class accommodation. Maximum speed was 90mph. The cars were the first on BR to be fully air-conditioned.

There were two power cars per set, built by Metropolitan-Cammell, each with a NBL/MAN 1,000hp engine powering two electric motors. The Swiss-designed Schlieren bogie was adapted as it had earned a good reputation on the Continent, but in practice, with the shorter British coach bodies, coupled with the weight of the traction motors, it proved rough riding.

The LMR's 'Birmingham Pullman' and the WR's 'Bristol Pullman' inaugurated in 1960, made two double runs each way daily. Rather uneconomically, the third WR set was held in reserve until 1961 when it became the 'South Wales Pullman'. Thenceforth, in the event of a 'Blue Pullman' being unavailable, a locomotive-hauled Pullman set was kept in reserve.

The 'Blue Pullmans' looked attractive in their initial blue and white livery with both ends streamlined, but were much less so after repainting into reverse livery. With the introduction of air conditioning in the far better riding MkIId standard coaches on B4 bogies, the Pullmans were withdrawn from service in the spring of 1973. None of these vehicles has survived.

⬆ The down 'Bristol Pullman' is seen west of Twerton Tunnel on 29 June 1964, the first day following an overhaul and repaint in original livery. Driving motor brake second (DMBS) No. W60098 is leading. *(Author)*

◥ The up 'Bristol Pullman' waits in the sunshine at Bristol
Temple Meads, ready to depart for Paddington on 8 August 1963.
DMBS No. W60099 leads. *(Author)*

◄ The up 'Bristol Pullman', now with a yellow front end, is
prepared for departure from Bristol Temple Meads on 5 June
1968. *(Author)*

◤ The down 'Bristol Pullman' catches the evening light west of
Twerton Tunnel on 3 April 1973, following a repaint into the less
attractive 'reverse' livery. *(Author)*

Class 253 InterCity 125 High Speed Train

The popular and familiar HST is often regarded as being a development of the Blue Pullmans. These trains are of course available to all ordinary ticket holders, with no supplement demanded. The HST uses the concept of a power car at each end, thus obviating the need to release a locomotive at the end of a journey for running round. This saves much time and occupation of track and ensures the train is ready for an almost immediate departure. The power cars have since been reclassified as locomotives and designated Class 43.

The coaches are air-conditioned MkIII stock with air-bag secondary suspension and disc brakes. Each power car had a Paxman Valenta 2,250hp engine driving an alternator providing power for the traction motors, but most have more recently been re-engined with MTU units of the same power. A significant advantage of an HST is its braking, which gives it the ability to run at 125mph within the signal spacings designed for 100mph.

Refurbished HSTs remain in front-line service to the West of England with First Great Western and CrossCountry.

⬅ A Paddington to Bristol Temple Meads HST crosses Brunel's St James's Bridge and enters Bath Spa station on 14 October 1977. It is in early livery – blue and light grey with yellow ends. Guards found that being located at the end of the power car was too noisy and so were later moved to the first coach. The guard's compartments have therefore since been removed from the power cars. The train is running in reverse order because the first-class coaches, with yellow band above the windows, were usually at the London end. A red band denoted refreshment facilities. *(Author)*

⬆ The 11.50 Bristol Temple Meads to Paddington HST set No. 253001, with power cars Nos 43002 and No 43003 at either end, accelerates through Bathampton on 10 May 1978. It is passing Class 46 'Peak' No. 46004 on an up freight held in the loop. *(Author)*

⬆ Ex-GWR diesel railcar No. W19W, in early BR livery, passes the signalbox at Ledbury on 16 May 1959. The driver and signalman are exchanging the single-line tablet. The station nameboard adds 'Junction for Gloucester', but this was no longer true when the branch closed to passengers on 11 July 1959. No. 19 was one of 38 diesel railcars used by the GWR. It was new in July 1940 and withdrawn in February 1960. *(R. E. Toop)*

GWR railcars and BR diesel multiple units

There had been various experiments with diesel-powered railcars prior to nationalisation, but it was only the GWR that was able to make any regular use of such vehicles. Following the formation of the Railway Executive and British Railways, an all-region committee was set up to investigate the possibilities of lightweight diesel passenger trains. The first order was placed with BR's Derby Carriage & Wagon Works with vehicles entering service in April 1954, which was before the BR Modernisation Plan of 1955.

The success of these early diesel multiple units (dmus) brought in some large orders, but with BR workshops already busy, many were constructed by independent companies as well as by Derby and Swindon works. This resulted in a variety of different couplings and electrical connections, although one of the main advantages of dmus was that two or more permanently formed sets of coaches could be coupled together and controlled by one driver. A system of colour coding was introduced with different colours and shapes marked on the ends of driving vehicles so that it was obvious which sets could be operated together. A total of nearly 4,000 of what were later regarded as first-generation dmus were built. Later classified under TOPS in the Class 1xx series, their ultimate replacement by more modern stock was a long-drawn-out process. It was not until the end of 2003 that the last of what had by then become known as 'Heritage' units were withdrawn from the Manchester area. Today, just two single-unit vehicles remain in operation on specific passenger duties, while many are usefully employed across the country on heritage railways.

⬆ Two three-car Gloucester Railway Carriage & Wagon Co. sets coupled together are framed by the signal gantry at Westbury on 29 September 1969. Class 119 driving motor brake second (DMBS) No. W51080 leads. The Gloucester-built units had standard Derby-pattern three window ends, but the Swindon-built Cross Country units had a more angular end with just two windows. The Trowbridge line is on the left and that to Newbury, right. A line of engineers' department wagons stand in the siding. *(Rev. Alan Newman)*

⬇ Derby Works-built Class 116 unit Nos W51137 and W51150 pass the former Staverton Halt on the Chippenham to Westbury line on 10 April 1970 with a down 'Railair' working. It consists of the two driving motor cars at each end with a pair of vans for luggage in between and is believed to have worked from Paddington to Hayes & Harlington, the nearest station to Heathrow Airport. This interesting combination of vehicles is rarely if ever seen today in model form. Staverton Halt closed on 18 April 1966 and the line was singled on 26 February 1967. *(Rev. Alan Newman)*

⬆ Some dmu vehicles were built with a driver's cab at both ends and were known as single-units or by their nickname 'bubblecars'. They could still be coupled to other compatible dmus to run as part of a longer train if required. Class 121 Pressed Steel DMBS No. W55033 is seen at Bristol Temple Meads on 23 April 1969 about to run to the small terminus at Severn Beach. This unit has survived into preservation at the Colne Valley Railway. *(Rev. Alan Newman)*

⬇ Derby Class 116 three-car set No. 353 arrives at Newport from Gloucester having just passed over the River Usk bridge and the ruins of Newport Castle on the right. The view was taken from the signalbox on 4 September 1972. *(Rev. Alan Newman)*

⬆ When the dmus were introduced in their dark green livery, men working on the track found it difficult to judge the speed of an approaching train as they were faster and quieter than their steam predecessors. To help them observe approaching trains, straw-coloured 'cat's whiskers' were painted on the ends, as seen here. Later, to make them even more obvious, large yellow panels were painted on the fronts and later still, all-over yellow ends were applied. A three-car Pressed Steel Class 117 set – with roof-mounted indicator panel – is seen near Sneyd Park on the Severn Beach to Bristol Temple Meads line *c*1960. *(Author's collection)*

⬇ Totnes station on 25 August 1975 with set No. P356 at the down platform. On the opposite side of the line is the now closed Unigate creamery which incorporated part of Brunel's atmospheric railway pumping station, now the subject of a preservation order. *(Rev. Alan Newman)*

➡ A three-car dmu approaches Westbury on 21 April 1966. The splendid array of semaphore signals has now long since gone. *(Rev. Alan Newman)*

◥ Swindon-built Class 120 DMSL (equipped with lavatory) No. W50662, leads a three-car Cross Country unit, as it nears Westbury from Trowbridge on 20 April 1968. It is in the later blue and light grey livery. *(Rev. Alan Newman)*

◁ Two three-car sets of Swindon Class 120 Cross Country units in green livery, with DMSL No. W50695 leading, form a down train at Heywood Junction, Westbury, on 29 July 1966. *(Rev. Alan Newman)*

↑ The rear view of a Swindon Cross Country unit leaving Bradford-on-Avon station in July 1966 and approaching the 159yd-long Bradford Tunnel. At this date, the notice on the right which read 'Warning to enginemen and firemen. Special care must be taken to prevent emission of smoke and fumes from engines at this place' was no longer necessary as all steam engines had been withdrawn from the area. *(Rev. Alan Newman)*

◤ Class 120 DMBC No. W50709 leaves Bradford-on-Avon station with a down train and drives into the sun on 19 July 1968. (*Rev. Alan Newman*)

◄ Swindon Cross Country unit DMBC No. W50737 heads a local service to Weston-super-Mare, passing Westmoreland Road yard, Bath. The sun glistens on the newly fallen snow, 3 February 1969. (*Rev. Alan Newman*)

▲ Swindon Cross Country Class DMBCs Nos W51576 and W51579 with intermediate trailer (TSL) No. W59582, approach Bathampton with an up train on 15 May 1969. Exhaust fumes have spoilt the effect of the recently whitened roof ends. (*Rev. Alan Newman*)

⬆ With dmus formed into permanent sets of two or three coaches, the Western Region applied set numbers to the ends of their trains. The three-figure number had a letter prefix denoting the area of operation, such as L for London, C for Cardiff and P for Plymouth. Bristol area-based Swindon Cross Country set No. B555 approaches Trowbridge on 6 June 1974 with a train to Bristol Temple Meads. This set comprised Class 120 vehicles Nos W51576, W59582 and W51590. *(Rev. Alan Newman)*

↗ A Class 120 Swindon unit in overall blue livery, emerges from the 159yd Bradford Tunnel onto Greenland Mill Crossing which is guarded by two half barriers, on 6 April 1968. *(Rev. Alan Newman)*

➡ Two Class 120 three-car sets, with No. B554 leading, leave Bradford-on-Avon with the 16.05 Weymouth to Bristol Temple Meads on 17 July 1972. *(Rev. Alan Newman)*

Another train is
coming if lights
continue to flash

178 BR Diesels in the 1960s and 1970s

◀ The Swindon InterCity Class 123 units, introduced in 1957, were unusual in having a gangway version of the glass-fibre front. They worked some Cardiff to Portsmouth services from 1963, but were later placed in store before being transferred to Hull. Here, two four-car sets, headed by DMBSL No. W52088, leave Bath Spa for Bristol Temple Meads on 1 July 1966. Semaphore signalling at the station changed to colour lights on 21 January 1968. *(Rev. Alan Newman)*

▲ Two four-car Class 123 InterCity sets arrive at Bradford-on-Avon on 15 April 1966 following a late snow fall. The leading car is DMSK (a side corridor vehicle with a lavatory) No. W52103. *(Rev. Alan Newman)*

A Derby 'Lightweight' dmu waits at Keswick on 18 August 1959. This type pre-dated the BR Modernisation Plan which heralded large numbers of dmus from various manufacturers. These early vehicles, numbered in the 79xxx series, had large side windows and cab windows through which front-seat passengers could enjoy an excellent view ahead. The impressive water tank and water crane date back to Cockermouth, Keswick & Penrith Railway days. A brazier for use in inclement weather ensures that the delivery pipe is not frozen. *(R. E. Toop)*

A Swindon InterCity dmu in green livery, but with a blue and light grey intermediate trailer, approaches Bradford-on-Avon with a Cardiff to Portsmouth train in November 1967. The goods shed, right, is worth a second glance. *(Rev. Alan Newman)*

↑ Single-unit No. B101 (Class 122 No. W55001 in departmental use as No. 975023) passes Bradford-on-Avon on crew-training duties on 21 November 1973. A GWR cast-iron trespass notice is displayed by the wicket gate to the left. *(Rev. Alan Newman)*

↗ In 1964, two green-liveried dmus on a down train west of Bathampton haul two maroon-liveried corridor coaches as a tail load. *(R. E. Toop)*

→ A three-car dmu is seen west of Bradford-on-Avon in January 1967. *(Rev. Alan Newman)*

AC Cars four-wheel railbus, BUT (AEC) 150bhp engine

In the author's opinion, the AC Cars railbus was the most attractive of the various designs of experimental four-wheel vehicles in the late 1950s. BR ordered a number of rail buses as an attempt to keep rural branch lines open by using a cheaper method of passenger transport than a locomotive and coaches on lines where even a full-length dmu would have been uneconomic. Railbuses were ordered from Bristol/Eastern Coach Works for the Scottish Region; Waggon Und Maschinenbau of Germany, for the Eastern Region; D. Wickham & Co. and Park Royal Vehicles, both for the Scottish Region, and AC Cars for the Western Region. At 11 tons the latter was the lightest vehicle, but seated only 46, the Bristol/ECW and German vehicles seating 56.

The AC Cars railbuses were allocated to Swindon for use on the Kemble, Tetbury and Cirencester branches.

Starting work on 2 February 1959 they offered a more intensive service than the steam trains they replaced and some new halts were opened. To keep costs as low as possible, these were at rail level, rather than the normal floor height. The railbuses carried the first conductor/guards to work on BR and this brought about further economy as it rendered station booking clerks and ticket collectors redundant.

Sometimes the railbuses suffered through overcrowding, particularly on the Cirencester branch, but replacement by a larger railcar would have increased operating costs. It would also have interfered with the cyclic working of the railbus in conjunction with the Tetbury branch. Despite support from the locality, these two branches were declared uneconomic and closed to passengers on 6 April 1964. Some railbuses were moved to the Yeovil Junction to Yeovil Town shuttle and on the Bodmin North to Boscarne Exchange Platform line. When these services were withdrawn, there were no other duties on which the AC railbuses would have been suitable. Two have been preserved.

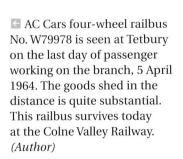

⬅ AC Cars four-wheel railbus No. W79978 is seen at Tetbury on the last day of passenger working on the branch, 5 April 1964. The goods shed in the distance is quite substantial. This railbus survives today at the Colne Valley Railway. *(Author)*

➡ On 10 August 1966 AC Cars No. W79978 is seen again, at the very short Boscarne Exchange Platform which enjoyed a very brief life, opening in 1964 and closing in 1967. The gradient board indicates a rising gradient of 1 in 250, steepening to 1 in 196. *(Author)*

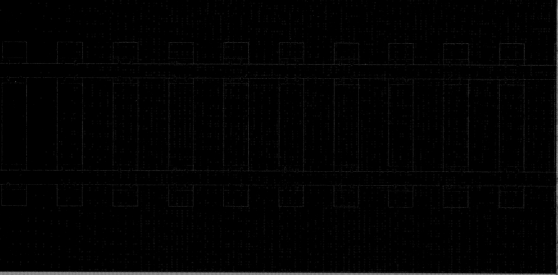

Southern Region diesel-electric multiple units

In the interests of standardisation with its electric stock, the Southern Region did not use dmus like those on the other regions, but adopted a demu design for use on non-electrified lines. With the engine driving through a generator rather than a gearbox, this equipment being larger required it to be placed above the floor, rather than slung below as with the dmus. They were fitted with the standard Eastleigh non-gangway cab front as used on electric trains.

The early six-car Hastings units had an English Electric 500hp motor coach at each end, but later units and the three-car Hampshire sets were fitted with an English Electric 600hp engine. Initially painted green, a large yellow 'V' was painted below the centre front window to increase visibility, perhaps not so pleasing aesthetically, but later the front was all yellow. The units had a good record of reliability, but the engines were rather noisy, giving rise to the sobriquet 'thumper'. A good number of vehicles from the various classes, 201 and 202 Hastings, 205 Hampshire and Berkshire, and 207 Oxted, survive in preservation.

⬆ Two Hastings six-car Class 203 (6B) demus, Nos 1034 and 1035 emerge from a mid-morning mist at Bradford-on-Avon with a Hastings to Weston-super-Mare special on 17 February 1973, well off their usual route. It was believed to have been organised to enable people to see potential summer holiday accommodation rather than to enjoy the off-season delights of this Somerset watering place. These units were built to a width of 8ft 2½in instead of the more general 9ft 3in in order to comply with the restricted loading gauge on the Hastings line. The train still displays the '54' which informs a signalman that it is a Victoria to Ore (not via Eastbourne) service. *(Rev. Alan Newman)*

⬆ Hampshire demu No. 1110 is seen at Salisbury curiously enough and appropriately on 11 October 1971 (11.10.71). The former GWR brick-built terminus is on the far right. *(Rev. Alan Newman)*

➡ Hampshire Class 205 (3H) three-car demu No. 1105 at Salisbury with the 11.46 to Portsmouth service on 15 February 1973. *(Rev. Alan Newman)*

⬆ Hampshire demu No. 1126 working the 11.18 Bristol Temple Meads to Portsmouth service, approaches Bradford-on-Avon on 9 June 1973. The stone wall is all that remains of the fine goods shed depicted on page 68. The dismantled good-quality stone would have been recycled. *(Rev. Alan Newman)*

↗ Class 205 demus Nos 1133 and 1132 forming the 11.18 Bristol Temple Meads to Portsmouth, approach Bradford-on-Avon in February 1974. These are Berkshire units – a luggage compartment replacing a second-class compartment in the similar Hampshire units. The headcode '85' indicates a Portsmouth & Southsea to Salisbury semi-fast service. *(Rev. Alan Newman)*

→ Reading to Redhill three-car 500hp Class 206 (3R) demu No. 1201 leaves Crowthorne on 31 January 1973. The driving trailer leads while exhaust fumes can be seen rising from the MBSO (motor brake second open) at the rear of the train. The power car and intermediate trailer were former Class 201 Hastings line stock, while the driving trailer was from a 2-EPB emu. This was therefore wider than the other two vehicles and so these sets became known as 'tadpoles'. Six were formed in 1964–5 for use on the Tonbridge–Reading line. *(Rev. Alan Newman)*

Electric locomotives

Class 76 (EM1), LNER/BR Bo-Bo 1,500V DC electric

58 built and introduced 1941 and 1950–3, Nos 26000–26057 (TOPS Nos 76001–76057)

A prototype electric locomotive, No. 6000 (BR No. 26000) was built by the LNER in 1941, for the Manchester to Sheffield electrification, but as this was suspended until the end of hostilities, the remainder of the class were not constructed until 1950–3.

Weighing 89 tons, these locomotives had a maximum speed of 65mph and proved exceptionally reliable. In later years the intervals between inspections and major maintenance were actually increased. The bogies carried both buffing and drawbar gear.

They were withdrawn with the closure of the 'Woodhead Route' across the Pennines in 1981, with one example retained in the National Collection.

Class 71 BR Bo-Bo 750V DC electric locomotive

24 built, introduced 1958–60, Nos E5000–E5023 (TOPS Nos 71001–71014)

These 77-ton locomotives were built at Doncaster Works for the Southern Region and allocated to Stewarts Lane depot. In addition to current collecting shoes, pantographs were fitted for use in freight yards where, for safety, it was necessary to install overhead wires. Rated at 2,552hp they could haul freight trains up to 900 tons in weight and passenger and fitted freight trains of 700 tons and had a maximum speed of 90mph. Ten were later rebuilt at Crewe Works as electro diesels, becoming Class 74. One example of Class 71 survives with the National Collection.

← Class 76 No. E26005 at Crewe Works on 8 June 1966. The 'E' prefix is unusual because it was applied erroneously at Crewe Works. For 26xxx and Class 77 27xxx numerals this was unnecessary because there were no steam locomotives with which they could have been confused. Crewe was well off the electrified route of these locomotives, hence the pantographs are down, but when it was electrified, it was at 25,000V AC!
(Rev. Alan Newman)

→ Class 71 No. E5011 in green livery waits at Victoria station ready to haul the 'Golden Arrow' to Dover on 14 April 1969.
(Author)

Class 73 BR/English Electric Bo-Bo electro diesel

49 built, introduced 1962–7, Nos E6001–E6049 (Initial TOPS Nos 73001–73006 and 73101–73142)

The 'EDs' (electro diesels) can take power from either the Southern's 750V DC third-rail supply, or from their on-board diesel engine. Extremely flexible, these 76-ton locomotives can work in multiple with other members of the class or with electric and diesel-electric multiple unit stock. Their purpose is to render the electrification of freight sidings unnecessary and to work trains over other non-electrified sections as well as maximising the use of the fixed power supply equipment on electrified lines. The driver can change from diesel to electric working while on the move. The collecting shoes are lowered by an air engine when electric operation is selected, and raised by springs when the diesel engine is required. Many remain in operation on the national network and on heritage railways.

← Class 73/1 'ED' No. E6042, in BR blue with yellow warning panel, stands at Brighton station on 11 August 1967. Later renumbered 73135 and 73235 for use on Gatwick Express trains. *(Rev. Alan Newman)*

↑ A line up of electro-diesels at Brighton on 7 August 1971: BR-built Class 73/0s Nos E6002 and E6006 and English Electric-built Class 73/1 No. E6020. The first six of the class were built at Eastleigh Works, the rest by EE at Vulcan Foundry. Positioning of the BR logo varied. *(Rev. Alan Newman)*

Electric
multiple units

An ex-LNER emu built by Metro-Cammell in 1937 for the Tyneside system waits at Whitley Bay station with its overall roof, in June 1967. The headcode indicates that it is a Newcastle to Newcastle train running via Heaton and Benton. The driver looks back awaiting the guard's 'Right away'. The lady on the platform holds the door open for the mother with the coach-built Silver Cross pram to join the train with her young family. Standing near the driver's compartment is a young lad dressed in ankle socks, sandals, short trousers and jacket, who is watching the photographer with interest. *(Author's collection)*

⬆ A Tyneside emu calls at Monkseaton on 1 August 1964 while working the 15.45 Newcastle to Newcastle service out via Benton and returning via Heaton. This 630V DC third-rail system connected Newcastle upon Tyne with North Shields and South Shields. The electrification was dispensed with in the 1960s with the emus replaced by dmus on sections not closed. Some lines are now part of the Tyne & Wear Metro system. These former LNER emus were articulated with the two cars sharing a common, central bogie, as can be seen here. *(Author's collection)*

⬇ Four-car 4-LAV emu No. 2925 leaves Brighton for Victoria on 26 August 1966. One trailer in each set had a side corridor with lavatory. The electrical equipment in these sets was of the standard suburban type, but the carriage bodies were of main line construction. *(Rev. Alan Newman)*

⬆ On the Southern Region 750V DC third-rail system, a pair of two-car 2-HAL emus, Nos 2652 and 2653, and one 2-BIL, head out from Brighton for Victoria on 26 August 1966. No. 2653 has a post-war all-steel driving trailer, the 'HAL' designation referring to 'half lavatory' as only this car had such a facility in each set. Driving trailers had a motorman's compartment, four first- and four third-class compartments connected to a lavatory while the motor coach contained the motorman's, guard's and seven third-class compartments only.

New features on these units, built at Eastleigh in 1938–9, were the driving ends which were built of welded rolled steel sections and panel plates, the windows flush with the sides, the driving end roofs were domed, and the doors of the motorman's compartment inset. The body consisted of steel panels on hardwood frames with a timber roof and floor. 'BIL' indicated that both coaches of each set had a side corridor and lavatory, but there was no connection between the coaches. *(Rev. Alan Newman)*

⬇ Four-car Class 420/1 4-BIG emu No. 7043 and Class 421/1 4-CIG No. 7323 near Angmering on 28 August 1968. *(Rev. Alan Newman)*

The four-car 4-COR units (corridor gangway throughout), were built in 1937 for the Southern Railway's electrification to Portsmouth. Each set comprised a 52-seat third-class open motor coach; a composite with three third-class and five first-class compartments, a third-class coach with eight compartments and a coupé, and a 52-seat third-class open motor coach. Both the intermediate trailers had lavatories at each end. Gangways were also provided at the driving ends so that passage throughout the train was available when two or more sets were coupled together. A passageway was fitted through the guard's compartment and a door fitted to the motorman's compartment. Sliding doors closed the corridor connection when not in use. The 4-CORs were nicknamed 'Nelsons' because as well as serving Portsmouth, one window at the front was blind. No. 3116 is seen at Seaford on 12 August 1970 with car 2-HAL No. 2604 on the right. *(Rev. Alan Newman)*

Class 421/2 4-CIG emu No. 7357 in blue and light grey livery, approaches Southease level crossing near Newhaven, working the 18.54 Brighton to Seaford on 14 August 1971. Southease signalbox doubled as a ticket and enquiry office. The platforms of Southease & Rodmell Halt are staggered. *(Rev. Alan Newman)*

The four-car Class 423 4-VEP (vestibule electro pneumatic) emus were designed for semi-fast services on the Southern Region. A set comprised a driving trailer containing a motorman's compartment, vestibule, second-class open saloon and three first-class side corridor compartments and a lavatory; a non-driving motor with a second-class open saloon, guard's compartment and luggage compartment; an open saloon trailer, and a driving trailer. The non-driving motor coach had four 250hp motors.

Nos 7787 and 7731 leave the ornate north portal of Clayton Tunnel on 31 July 1971. It is most unusual for an inhabited cottage to be situated immediately above the tunnel mouth as here. *(Rev. Alan Newman)*

London Transport stock

London Transport electrified lines differ from most others as they use the fourth-rail system, with the negative rail in the centre and the positive to the side. Stock is of two types: low height for use in tube tunnels and standard height for normal tunnels.

◄ The Ongar three-car shuttle train of pre-1938 stock terminates at Epping on 10 March 1962. A connecting Central Line train is on the left. *(Author)*

⬆ A District Line train of R stock from Wimbledon enters East Putney station on 28 May 1968 with car No. 21108 leading. *(Rev. Alan Newman)*

⬇ Battery service locomotive No. 18 and Bo-Bo electric locomotive No. 12 *Sarah Siddons* at Neasden on 6 June 1971. Former Metropolitan Railway No. 12 was built in 1922 by Vickers and has been retained as a working museum piece. *(Rev. Alan Newman)*

Isle of Wight electric trains

Restricted clearances on the Isle of Wight meant that dieselisation would be difficult and expensive as no standard locomotives or multiple units could be used without expensive alteration. London Transport had ex-Northern Line tube stock available at the time, which fitted the Isle of Wight loading gauge and so the 8½ miles of line from Ryde Pier Head to Shanklin were electrified at a cost of approximately half a million pounds. The cars were converted from four- to three-rail 630V DC electrification with services commencing on 20 March 1967. As the floors of the ex-tube stock were lower than the station platforms, it proved more convenient to raise the track level in stations rather than lower the platforms, the exception being at Ryde Esplanade.

The 43 cars purchased from London Transport dated back to the 1920s and were formed into six four-car sets of Class 485 (4-VEC) comprising a motor, two trailers and a motor car, and six three-car sets of Class 486 (3-TIS) comprising a motor, trailer and driving trailer. One motor car was held as a spare. Each motor car had two 240hp motors with a maximum speed of 46mph.

The winter service used two four-car sets on weekdays and one on Sundays, while in summer, trains were formed of a 4-VEC + 3-TIS. The three-car sets were not used singly as the current collecting shoes were only at one end. Having become the oldest carriages in regular use on the national network they were replaced in 1989 by further conversions from LT trains of more up-to-date, 1938, stock.

⬆ A former London Transport emu in operation on the Isle of Wight system as No. 034, seen on Ryde Pier, 5 May 1977. *(Rev. Alan Newman)*

Index

Photographic locations

Locomotives depicted

Diesel